GOOD
HOUSEKEEPING

SIMPLE CLEANING WISDOM

GOOD HOUSEKEEPING

SIMPLE CLEANING WISDOM

450 EASY SHORTCUTS FOR A FRESH & TIDY HOME

EDITED BY CAROLYN FORTÉ

HEARST
books

2

28

54

80

110

132

148

CONTENTS

INTRODUCTION | 1

CHAPTER 1
CLEANING BASICS | 2

CHAPTER 2
THE KITCHEN | 28

CHAPTER 3
LAUNDRY & CLOTHING CARE | 54

CHAPTER 4
BEDROOMS, FAMILY ROOMS &
HOME OFFICES | 80

CHAPTER 5
THE BATHROOM | 110

CHAPTER 6
THE GARAGE & OUTDOOR SPACES | 132

CHAPTER 7
STAIN RESCUE | 148

PHOTO CREDITS | 194

INDEX | 196

LET'S GET CLEANING!

Most of us have a love-hate relationship with "keeping house." I know I do. I love a clean home and the feeling of calm it brings my family, but I hate the dusting, mopping, scrubbing, and wiping needed to get it that way. Yes, there are those who really do *enjoy* cleaning, but if you're like me, it's just one more responsibility in an already packed day and something I try to accomplish as quickly as possible.

Well, that's about to change. Whether you're a novice or a pro, an enthusiast or a procrastinator, you're in luck. *Good Housekeeping Simple Cleaning Wisdom* is jam-packed with Good Housekeeping Institute Lab–tested products and speedy, smart tricks and tips to help you clean faster, declutter more easily, tackle trouble spots, simplify big jobs, and accomplish more in less time. And who doesn't want (and need) more free time?

In some chapters, you'll find a checklist of what chores to do when and the go-to cleaning products and tools *Good Housekeeping* recommends for every household. We also dive deep, devoting entire chapters to the kitchen, living spaces, bathroom, laundry and clothing care, and more. You'll find advice about how to keep your appliances working their best; how to zap dust, germs, and other allergens; how to make your bathroom sparkle when guests are at the door; and even how to wash special-care items, like pillows and comFortérs. As you read along, keep an eye out for recurring features, like GH Lab–tested products that carry the trusted Good Housekeeping Seal, common mistakes to avoid, and the ultraspeedy 1-Minute Tips.

Because a home should look as good on the outside as it does on the inside, you'll also find shortcuts for cleaning the deck, patio, garage, gutters, windows, and even the car. Clean, organized, guest-ready outdoor areas make a home feel larger and boost its value and curb appeal. Not a bad payoff for a little extra effort!

Cleaning your home is really about caring for your home. And caring for your home is really about caring for your family. *Good Housekeeping* has a long tradition of caring for American homes and families, and every hint tucked into these pages was put there to help you take better care of your family. And if you look at it that way, what's not to love about cleaning? Please enjoy!

—Carolyn Forté
Director of Home Appliances,
Cleaning Products, and Textiles Labs
Good Housekeeping

A LITTLE GOES A LONG WAY

Spend five or 10 minutes daily doing
simple tasks like sorting mail, picking
up clutter, and wiping down appliances,
countertops, and shower walls. You'll
delay (or maybe even eliminate) the need
for deep-cleanings and make them easier
to do if and when the time comes.

CLEANING BASICS

"I make no secret of the fact that I would rather lie on a sofa than sweep beneath it."

—*Shirley Congran, novelist*

Keeping a clean, healthy home is one of the most important ways to care for your family, and it's easier to do than it might seem. In the pages that follow, we'll recommend the best tools and products to use, when it's time to do what tasks, and even ways to clean up after messy kids and pets. And we've sprinkled in lots of smart shortcuts to help you get a clean, tidy home with time to spare. Let's get started!

PRO CLEANER HABITS YOU SHOULD TOTALLY STEAL

For professional housekeepers, time is money.
Put that same approach to work in your home.

KEEP SUPPLIES HANDY

Stock a cleaning caddy with essentials, like rubber gloves, paper towels, a small brush, and your favorite cleaners, to save time and stay organized. Try individual caddies with tools for the kitchen, bathrooms, bedrooms, and living areas, stashing them in each room and safely out of children's reach.

BANISH CLUTTER BEFORE YOU CLEAN UP

Recycle newspapers and magazines you won't read, and put shoes back where they belong (or have their owners do it!). Clear kitchen and bathroom counters so surfaces are easier to get to and you don't waste time moving or cleaning around things that aren't where they belong.

WORK FROM TOP TO BOTTOM

Dust first, then vacuum to keep dust and
dirt from falling onto the surface you've
already cleaned. Always leave your floors
for last and clean your way out of the room.

HAVE "HOUSE ONLY" SHOES

Taking shoes off at the door helps keep dirt outside. Designate slippers or soft-sole footwear as inside shoes, and floors and carpets will stay cleaner longer.

LET YOUR CLEANER DO THE WORK

Ever watch a hotel housekeeper clean? She'll spray a surface with cleaner, go tackle another task while the formula dissolves the dirt and then come back several minutes later to wipe the surface clean without scrubbing. Smart!

CLEANING NO-NO'S

Avoid these common mistakes and you'll shave precious minutes off your cleaning routine.

VACUUMING BARE FLOORS WITH A ROTATING BRUSH

Not only can spinning bristles damage a wood floor, they can scatter debris, making it harder to collect. For bare floors, use a canister with a bare-floor brush or a stick vacuum. If an upright is your only option, switch off the brush.

SPRAYING POLISH DIRECTLY ON FURNITURE

Spraying polish on your cloth is the way to go if you want to avoid a filmy buildup that attracts more dust.

WASHING WINDOWS ON A SUNNY DAY

Pick a cloudy day to do this job or start on the shady side of the house. Spraying window cleaner directly on hot windows causes it to dry too quickly before you can wipe it away, leaving hard-to-remove streaks behind.

USING DIRTY CLEANING TOOLS

Dirty, ragged cloths, mops, and scrubbers don't work as efficiently as clean, well-kept tools do. Clean or replace your tools often, so they are up to the task.

1-MINUTE TIP! Foaming cleaners cling to vertical surfaces, like walls and windows, better than thin sprays do, so they dissolve more dirt in less time. Look for sprays that dispense as foam.

CLEANUP CALENDAR

Follow our suggestions or write up your own lists of
must-do chores that are most important to you.

KITCHEN

Make these tasks part of your regular routine to keep
your home looking great 24/7.

DAILY

- Dispose of trash and recyclables.
- Hand-wash and dry dishes or load them into the dishwasher.
- Wipe down table, countertops, and range top.
- Wash coffeemaker after each use.
- Clean the sink.
- Sweep or vacuum floor, if needed.

WEEKLY

- Clean your kitchen appliances. Wipe down the range top, including burners, knobs, and backsplash, along with the oven front, handle, and range hood. Wipe microwave inside and out.
- Organize refrigerator and wipe spills on shelves and in bins; dispose of leftover foods that have spoiled or won't be eaten.
- Clean countertop items; move them away from walls and clean under and behind them.
- Wipe table and chairs.
- Vacuum and wash the floor.

OCCASIONAL

- Wipe refrigerator sides and top, and vacuum the coils.
- Wash refrigerator shelves and bins.
- Clean ventilating fan/ hood filters.
- Clean cabinets and drawers.
- Dust or vacuum woodwork.
- Wash curtains, windows, screens, blinds, and shades.
- Clean light fixtures.
- Clean the oven.

BATHROOM

These simple steps will ensure that your bathroom is always guest-ready.

DAILY

- Use a squeegee on tile walls and glass doors after showering.
- Wipe mirrors, faucets, and countertops.
- Straighten towels.
- Sweep or vacuum the floor, if needed.

WEEKLY

- Scrub bathtubs and sinks and wipe tile surfaces and countertops.
- Clean toothbrush holders and soap dishes.
- Clean shower stalls and doors.
- Clean toilets.
- Vacuum and wash floors.

OCCASIONALLY

- Wash throw rugs and shower curtains.
- Wash curtains, windows, screens, blinds, and shades.
- Clean and organize medicine cabinet; properly dispose of expired medicines.
- Clean light fixtures.
- Dust walls and woodwork.

ALL THROUGH THE HOUSE

Don't sweat it! Just do what you can, when you can. Eventually, it all gets done.

DAILY

- Put shoes, books, toys, clothing, and other stray items where they belong.
- Straighten living spaces and bedrooms.
- Make beds.
- Go through mail, newspapers, and magazines, and recycle what's not needed.

WEEKLY

- Dust furniture, mirrors, picture frames, lamps, and electronics.
- Vacuum floors, upholstery, and woodwork.
- Wipe smudges off walls and woodwork.
- Empty wastepaper baskets. Change bed linens.
- Recycle newspapers older than one week and magazines older than three months.

OCCASIONALLY

- Clean curtains and draperies; vacuum radiators and heating/cooling vents.
- Wash windows, screens, blinds, and shades.
- Deep-clean rugs and carpets; wash floors.
- Straighten closets; donate unused items.
- Clean and tidy garage, basement, and attic.
- Clean humidifiers, dehumidifiers, and fans, as needed.
- Clean display cabinets, bookcases, and contents of each.

MUST-HAVE CLEANING TOOLS

The GH Cleaning Lab promises that these eight tools will take care
of virtually all your cleaning tasks.

1 **SQUEEGEE.** Hang one from the showerhead or tile wall in each bathroom. Make it a rule that the last one out of the shower wipes down the walls; you'll keep mold and mildew away for months. **Casabella® Clip-On Silicone Squeegee** is comfortable to hold, and the silicone blade nabs every drop.

2 **MICROFIBER CLOTHS.** These cloths can be used wet or dry to grab dust, dirt, and grease from surfaces without leaving streaks or lint behind. Plus, they are washable and reusable. Use different colors for different rooms and tasks. **Weiman® Microfiber Cloth for Stainless Steel** is double-sided to clean and polish stainless-steel appliances to a showroom shine.

3 **VACUUM CLEANER.** A good vacuum cleaner is your go-to tool for cleaning carpets, bare floors, upholstery, lampshades, woodwork, and more in a hurry. Keep several types (upright, stick, and handheld) for different uses, and stash them where they will be handy.

Miele® Upright and Canister Vacuums use high-filtration bags and filters and are supereffective at picking up dirt and keeping it inside the vacuum. A plus for allergy sufferers!

4 **SCRUBBERS.** A sturdy scrub brush with natural or synthetic bristles is a must-have to remove tough, stuck-on soils. Stock an array of smaller brushes for dishes, bathrooms, and hard-to-reach nooks and crannies, like door tracks and tile grout. Keep both delicate and tough scrubber sponges on hand for cookware.

Eraser-type pads, like **Mr. Clean® Magic Eraser**, are best for cleaning crayon, scuffs, and other marks from walls and floors.

5 **PAPER TOWELS.** In addition to soaking up spills, these disposable sheets are perfect for messy jobs or for lining refrigerator bins and pantry shelves to absorb drips.

Bounty® Paper Towels always come out on top in absorbency and wet and dry durability tests.

6 **DUSTERS.** Disposable electrostatic dusters (like GH Seal–holder **Swiffer®**) or washable and reusable microfiber ones with short handles for furniture and long, extendable handles for floors, light fixtures, ceiling fans, bookcases, and other hard-to-reach places are the easiest and quickest way to zap dirt and dust from delicate surfaces without having to drag out the vacuum or climb a ladder.

7 **FLOOR MOP.** Whether you prefer a separate mop and bucket, a steam mop, or an all-in-one spray mop system, wet cleaning is key to keeping wood, tile, vinyl, and stone floors sparkling. Mopping keeps floors free of stains and the fine, abrasive grit that damages floors and that vacuums can miss.

Swiffer® Bissell® SteamBoost™ Steam Mop is a floor steamer that also uses disposable cleaner-filled pads. In our tests, it removed dirt and stains from vinyl and tile in one swipe without leaving any sticky residue behind.

8 **RUBBER GLOVES.** Nothing protects your hands (and manicure) while cleaning and doing dishes like a sturdy pair of rubber gloves. Make them serve double duty to get a grip on a stuck jar lid or even help hold on to a hot lobster. Dampened, they easily gather pet hair off a couch. Keep separate pairs for cleaning and the kitchen.

Playtex® Living® Gloves are durable, easy to take on and off, and have extra-long cuffs to keep sleeves and arms dry.

MUST-HAVE CLEANERS

Pare down to these seven essentials and end cleaning-cabinet clutter once and for all.

1 **DISINFECTING WIPES.** These time-savers make quick work of killing germs on kitchen and bathroom surfaces and frequently touched spots, like light switches, doorknobs, and remote controls. For maximum germ killing, be sure to follow label directions and keep surfaces wet for the required time.

2 **GLASS MULTI-SURFACE CLEANER.** This powerhouse is not only strong enough to cut grease on stovetops, but it also wipes away easily, leaving mirrors and glass streak-free, too. **Windex® Disinfectant Cleaner Multi-Surface** powers through marks on painted walls, countertops, and glass and is formulated to kill germs, too.

5 **KITCHEN AND BATHROOM CLEANER.** An all-purpose cleaner that works in of both these rooms saves space in your cleaning cabinet. Look for one that's as tough on grease as it is on soap scum.

CLR® Bath & Kitchen Cleaner cuts through tough stains and leaves grout whiter than other cleaners tested.

3 **FLOOR CLEANER.** If a mop and bucket is your style, a good liquid floor cleaner is a must. Dilute ¼ cup in one gallon of water for cleaning without the need to rinse. For wood floors, choose a cleaner made for wood, and don't overwet or wet-clean them more than necessary. Too much water can damage wood.

Mr. Clean Multi-Purpose Cleaner with the Scent of Gain can be diluted for big jobs or used full-strength on a sponge for quick surface cleaning.

6 **TOILET BOWL CLEANER.** Easiest and neatest for this icky job are disposable (or flushable) scrubbers with built-in cleaner that you just scrub and toss. If you prefer a separate cleaner and brush, keep germs at bay by letting the brush dry before placing it back in the holder. Be sure to clean the caddy often, too.

4 **DISH DETERGENTS.** Hand- and automatic-dishwashing detergents are two separate products and should never be used interchangeably. Hand-washing liquids are way too sudsy to be used in the dishwasher but are mild enough to remove stains from clothing and carpeting and for hand-washing delicate fabrics. Automatic-dishwashing detergents are just for use in the dishwasher.

Cascade® Platinum ActionPacs handle even the toughest baked-on mac 'n' cheese messes with ease and leave glasses crystal clear.

7 **FURNITURE POLISH.** Abrasive dust particles can damage your wood furniture's finish, and feather dusters just spread dust around. Use polish to dampen your cloth for scratch-free dusting. To avoid a filmy buildup, spray the cloth, not the wood, and buff with a dry cloth.

Guardsman® Anytime Clean & Polish cleans well and doesn't streak.

 1-MINUTE TIP! Clean stainless steel appliances in the direction of the metal's grain. Wipe in circles and you'll leave hard-to-remove streaks behind.

VACUUM CLEANER SMARTS

What to know to buy the best vacuums for your cleaning needs.

CANISTER Best for: homes with mostly bare floors, low-pile carpets, and stairs. It may come with or without a power nozzle rotating brush attachment for cleaning deep-pile carpets and offers greater flexibility than an upright when vacuuming tight spaces.

HANDHELD Best for: localized pickups of small dry or wet messes on hard surfaces, like spilled cereal or potting soil, or cleaning the car. Most are rechargeable and run for 15 minutes or more.

STICK Best for: light in-between cleanings of bare floors and low-pile carpets. They are lightweight, easy to carry and store, and come corded or cordless. Some cordless models can run for 45 minutes or longer.

UPRIGHT Best for: homes with wall-to-wall carpeting, large rugs, and no stairs. It loosens and removes embedded dirt better than other types of vacs but may be heavy. Most models come with onboard tools and hoses for above-the-floor cleaning.

ROBOT Best for: reaching under furniture and other spots you never get to. These new kids on the vacuum block can be scheduled to clean while you are out, and many go back to the charger when they're done. Most do a thorough job and can extend the time between deep-cleanings.

GIVE THAT CLEANER SOME TLC

Keep your vacuum in tip-top shape by avoiding
these four common care mistakes.

1 WAITING TOO LONG TO CHANGE THE BAG
Even though some vacs have "check bag" indicators, don't rely on them. Check the bag yourself and change it when it's three-quarters full to keep pickup at its peak. If you have a bagless model, empty the dust cup after every two to three uses.

2 NOT WASHING OR CHANGING THE FILTER
Dirty filters can't do their primary job—trapping allergens. Follow your owner's manual and change or wash the filters, usually every six months or as recommended. Your whole family will breathe easier.

3 REWINDING THE CORD HAPHAZARDLY
Merely pressing the REWIND button and letting the retractable cord snap back into place can send it off its track and you to the repair shop. Instead, hold the cord in your hand as you press the pedal to carefully wind it back into the vacuum.

4 NOT CLEANING THE BRUSH ROLL A brush roll that doesn't turn doesn't clean, and the stress of tangled hair and threads in the bristles can burn out the motor. To prevent this, unwind or snip away any tangles. Check your manual or your brand's website for instructions on how to remove the brush roll, if necessary, for cleaning. Good Housekeeping Lab pick **Electrolux® Precision® Brushroll Clean** vacuums have hidden blades that, with the push of a button, slice through threads and hair twisted around the brush, pulling them right into the dust cup.

PANTRY STAPLES THAT CLEAN HOUSE, TOO!

DISTILLED WHITE VINEGAR

has so many uses around the house that there are now stronger "cleaning vinegars" you can buy. Use it to de-gunk showerheads and dissolve hard water minerals on fixtures and glassware. Set out in a bowl or simmered on the stove, it neutralizes cooking odors so your home won't smell like bacon or fish.

BAKING SODA

makes a great deodorizer for fabrics, the fridge, and even the drain and can be used to shine stainless-steel sinks and chrome. On a damp rag, it removes scuffs from floors.

SALT

is a mild abrasive that, when combined with lemon juice, makes a great copper-cleaning scrub. Sprinkle it on fresh wine or grease spills on carpets and fabrics to absorb the mess before it soaks in.

LEMON JUICE

can help remove rust stains from fabrics and surfaces and is a great grease cutter. Toss lemon rind slivers and ice cubes in the garbage disposal to deodorize and de-gunk the blades. Add lemon juice to a bowl of water and nuke for 5 minutes to freshen your microwave.

CLEANING UP AFTER KIDS

Little ones can create big messes. Here's help to restore order.

TACKLE THEIR PLAYTHINGS

Bins are an easy way for kids to get to and put back toys. Stash some pretty ones around the house where toy clutter accumulates. Remind kids that they must refill the basket when playtime is over.

WIPE AWAY WALL DOODLES

When your child uses the walls as a canvas, erase crayon marks with a damp sponge dipped in baking soda. Or a pass with **Mr. Clean Magic Eraser** will remove their latest artwork.

USE THE DISHWASHER

Hard plastic toys (without electronic components) can be cleaned in the dishwasher. Place them securely in the top rack and choose the Normal cycle.

 1-MINUTE TIP! Use a sticky lint roller to quickly pick up spilled glitter, confetti, and residue from other kid crafting mishaps.

FRESHEN STUFFED ANIMALS

Rub plush toys with baking soda, then vacuum them to remove stale odors. Washable ones can be placed in a pillowcase to be washed and dried on the delicate cycle.

CLEANING UP AFTER PETS

Furry family members present cleaning challenges all their own.
Tackle the smell and the mess, fast.

COLLECT FUR

Spray upholstery fabric and carpeting with an antistatic spray, like **Static Guard®**, to break the charge that causes fur to cling to these surfaces. That will make the fur easier to gather or vacuum up.

MANAGE MUDDY PAWPRINTS

Resist the urge to mop up mud the minute pets track it in. It will be easier to vacuum from floors and carpets if you let it dry. Gather dry dirt from floors with a handheld vacuum or dust pan and brush, then wipe with a wet paper towel.

FIGHT SMELLS

Baking soda comes to the rescue once again! Sprinkle pet beds, litter boxes, rugs, and even Fido himself with baking soda, brushing it into the surface of his coat. Wait 15 minutes, then vacuum or brush again. **Febreze® Fabric Pet Odor Eliminator** actually traps and removes odor molecules so they are gone for good. It doesn't just cover them up.

ERASE STAINS

Not only are accidents on carpets and upholstery unsightly, but they retain odors that draw pets back to the scene of the crime. Zap them with a cleaner that contains enzymes to remove the stains and odors that keep pets coming back. **Bissell Professional Pet Stain and Odor Removing Formula** is safe for use on carpeting, upholstery, and water-safe surfaces, like mattresses.

KEEP IT SIMPLE

White kitchens are timeless, but every kitchen is more inviting and easier to clean with uncluttered counters and pared-down decor.

chapter

2

THE KITCHEN

"The best way to get rid of kitchen odors: Eat out."

—*Phyllis Diller, comedian*

No matter what its size, your kitchen is, no doubt, the heart of your home. You cook there, eat there, work there, and friends and family gather there. To help keep it a warm and welcoming place, this chapter is filled with tips and product recommendations to clean up in a hurry; keep your appliances humming; rescue burned cookware; tend to floors, cabinets, and counters; and even take steps to keep germs and odors under control.

30 MINUTES TO A SPARKLING KITCHEN

These shortcuts will have this room clean and organized in no time.

1 **CLEAR THE COUNTER.** A cluttered kitchen looks like a dirty kitchen, even if it's not. Plus, clutter cuts down on valuable workspace. Relocate mail and papers to a home-office area and rarely used small appliances to upper cupboards or other closets. Wipe counters with an all-purpose product, like Good Housekeeping Lab pick **Mr. Clean Multi-Purpose Cleaner with Gain Original Fresh Scent**. It makes quick work of cutting grease and grime.

2 **DON'T FORGET THE TABLE.** Like countertops, the kitchen table can easily become a dumping ground. Keep it "set" with placemats and a bowl of fruit or vase of flowers so family members will be less likely to drop items there. Set up other areas nearby to stash takeout menus, coupons, invites, and bills. Use desk organizers to keep them tidy and off the table.

3 **SPOT-CLEAN THE STOVETOP.**
Wipe spills, crumbs, and grease splatters with a multipurpose cleaner and a cloth or a sponge well-wrung in hot water. For burned-on bits, use a scrubber sponge dipped in baking soda. Wipe clean.

4 **WIPE DOWN APPLIANCES.**
With a dampened microfiber cloth, go over the handles and fronts of your oven, dishwasher, and refrigerator to get rid of fingerprints and sticky spots. Open the doors slightly and wipe any obvious drips along the edges.

Weiman Stainless Steel Cleaner & Polish Aerosol not only lifts dirt; it helps stainless-steel appliances resist fingerprints, too.

5 **STRAIGHTEN THE SINK.** Load stray items into the dishwasher. Rinse and wipe drippy detergent bottles, and relocate extra scrubbers, brushes, and rubber gloves under the sink. De-gunk the hand soap dispenser with a hot-water rinse, and wipe up any water that's splashed onto the faucet and surrounding area.

6 **TACKLE THE FLOOR.** Just dampen a paper towel and use it to erase any noticeable spills or stains. Dip it in a little baking soda to rub out scuffs; wipe dry. Use a disposable sweeper.

Swiffer Sweeper grabs dust, hair, and fine crumbs in a hurry. Swiffer wet cloths dissolve stuck-on grime in just a few passes.

FOR STONE COUNTERTOPS,

Weiman Granite & Stone Cleaner & Polish Spray is ideal. In lab tests, it left granite, marble, and quartz surfaces clean and shiny.

TLC FOR YOUR APPLIANCES

Keeping these kitchen powerhouses clean helps them work better and last longer.

PROTECT YOUR INVESTMENT

Major appliances are among the most expensive items in your kitchen. Keeping them in tip-top shape is easy and smart! For the quickest removal, tackle grime before it dries on.

THE REFRIGERATOR

STAY ON TOP OF SPILLS

Wipe drippy bottles before putting them back in the fridge, and sop up drips before they become caked on. Removable, washable shelf liners and mini bins make cleanup quick and easy and keep you from having to empty the entire fridge to clean it. When parts do need cleaning, wash them in the sink in warm, sudsy water. Clean the gasket folds, door handles, and front panels with a warm, sudsy sponge and rinse. Or use a stainless-steel cleaner, like **Weiman Stainless Steel Cleaner & Polish Aerosol.**

KEEP TRACK OF LEFTOVERS

Forgotten food stuck way in the back causes odors that can transfer to other foods and even ice. Use tight-sealing storage containers, like **Snapware® Total Solution™ Pyrex® Glass Containers**. Trash day or your next trip to the grocery store is a good time to toss anything that won't be eaten or past its prime. Keep smells in check with a fresh box of baking soda. Replace it every three months.

VACUUM THE COILS

Dusty coils make your refrigerator work harder and can put a strain on the condenser. Every three to four months, clean coils of dust with your vacuum's crevice tool, its dusting brush attachments, or a special coil-cleaning brush. Coils may be located on top, underneath, or in the back of your refrigerator, depending on the style. Check your manual or with the manufacturer to be sure. Remove and wash the drip tray under the refrigerator every other month or as dust and hair collects there, too.

THE RANGE

FILTER CHECK

Every few months, pop out the removable mesh filter from your kitchen's exhaust hood and either wash it in the dishwasher (if your brand recommends it) or swish it in a sink of hot sudsy water. Rinse, dry, and replace.

CLEAN THE GRATES

Wash porcelain and cast-iron gas range cooking grates in the sink in warm, sudsy water. After washing cast-iron grates, coat them with a thin layer of cooking oil and bake for 10 minutes at 350°F to "season" them.

WIPE STILL-WARM MESSES

Before you sit down to dinner, wipe range-top spills with a cloth or sponge. They'll be easier to remove before they dry.

SELF-CLEAN THE OVEN

Do this whenever the oven gets dirty, otherwise built-up, burned-on spills will smoke and smell during cleaning. Turn on the exhaust fan and open a window to help purge odors.

DEGREASE THE GLASS

Between cleanings, go over the oven-door glass with a window cleaner and a delicate scrubbing pad. Rinse and dry.

PICK THE RIGHT PRODUCT

In Good Housekeeping Institute tests, **Weiman's range cleaners** removed baked-on soil from gas and smooth-top ranges with little effort. There's **Gas Range Cleaner & Degreaser, Cook Top Daily Cleaner Spray**, and the **Glass Cook Top Cleaning Kit**. Choose the one most appropriate for your style of appliance.

GOOD HOUSEKEEPING

THE DISHWASHER

RINSE THE FILTER

Food particles trapped in the filter keep your dishwasher from cleaning as well as it could. Remove any large debris, like pasta or beans, when you see them. Every month or so, remove the filter from the bottom of the machine, rinse it well under hot water, scrub it with a soft brush if necessary, and reinsert it.

PREVENT ODORS

To keep odors at bay, don't let dishes with caked-on food sit in the machine. If you're not running a cycle right away, rinse dirty dishes in the sink, or turn on the Rinse-Only cycle and prop open the dishwasher door when it's done to air it out and help moisture evaporate.

RUN A CLEANING CYCLE

Theoretically, your dishwasher gets clean whenever you run a cycle, but residue and water minerals can build up inside. To purge them, fill a small bowl with 2 cups of distilled white vinegar and place it in the bottom rack of an empty dishwasher. Run a Normal cycle (without detergent or heated dry). Or use a dishwasher cleaner monthly in place of detergent in an empty machine. **Cascade Dishwasher Cleaner** washes away stains and trapped food bits and removes odors.

5 TIPS TO CLEANER DISHES

1 Purge cold water from the pipes by running hot water at the sink before starting the cycle. The hotter the water is, the better cleaning you'll get.

2 Nestle glasses between tines, not over them, to prevent spotting. Angle glasses and cups so water drains and doesn't puddle in bottom wells.

3 Load dishes with the dirtiest sides facing down, toward the center or where the water spray is strongest. Place platters and trays along the side or back, not where they can interfere with the opening of the detergent dispenser. Avoid cramming or overlapping items. If water can't reach something, it won't get clean.

4 If your flatware goes in a basket (instead of a top tray), load forks pointing up, knives down, and spoons alternating up and down for best cleaning and to prevent nesting.

5 If you use a detergent tablet, place it in the dispenser, not in the bottom of the tub. Otherwise, it can dissolve too quickly and get washed away before the main wash cycle starts

COUNTERTOP APPLIANCES

Keep these small kitchen helpers clean, too, so they are
up to the task when you need them.

DAILY UPKEEP

These mini kitchen dynamos often get
more use than your major appliances, and
have more nooks and crannies to trap food
and germs. Clean them regularly or after
each use, if needed.

THE MICROWAVE

1 FRESHEN WITH LEMONS.
Put one cup of water in a microwave-safe bowl. Add several lemon slices for a nice scent. Microwave on HIGH for 5 minutes. The steam will soften any dried-on mess so it can be wiped away with a sponge.

2 CLEAN HIDDEN SPOTS.
Remove the turntable and wash it by hand or in the dishwasher. Wipe the oven bottom, the inside of the door, and the doorframe to be sure it closes tightly. For the exterior, spray a cloth or sponge with cleaner and wipe the controls and door button. Rinse.

3 ZAP BURNED ODORS.
When burned popcorn and other odors linger too long, eliminate them by placing one cup of distilled white vinegar in a microwave-safe bowl inside the oven and boil it on High for 5 minutes. You can also place an absorbent, like **Fresh Wave® Gel** or **Packs**, inside the oven overnight. They use plant extracts to neutralize odor molecules.

 1-MINUTE TIP! Stash a paper plate close to the microwave to use as a cover when reheating food. It catches splatters better than a paper towel and makes for easy or no cleanup. If it's dirty and not reusable, just toss it.

THE COFFEEMAKER

1 **WASH IT DAILY.** Just rinsing the carafe of a drip coffeemaker is not enough. Coffee oils, if not washed away, can build up and give coffee an off flavor. Disassemble and wash the carafe, lid, and basket daily in hot sudsy water or in the dishwasher. Use a delicate scrubber sponge to remove deposits inside the glass carafe or add a big handful of rice to the sudsy water and swirl. For single-serve coffeemakers, wash the drip tray and wipe the reservoir and "pod" chamber of splatters and loose grinds.

2 **DE-SCALE IT.** Three or four times a year, fill the reservoir with a 50/50 mix of distilled white vinegar and water. Insert a paper filter and brew until the reservoir is half empty. Let sit 30 minutes or up to several hours, then finish brewing the vinegar. Fill the reservoir with clear water and brew until empty to rinse and remove any vinegar traces. For single-serve machines, use full-strength vinegar or follow the manufacturer's directions.

3 **REPLACE THE FILTERS.** Stock up on any water filters your brewer uses and replace them bimonthly or as your brand recommends.

4 **LEAVE THE LID UP.** Germs love moisture, so between uses, open the lid of the empty water chamber to help keep bacteria and mold from growing.

PURGE THE RESERVOIR REGULARLY.

If you haven't used your coffeemaker in more than one week, "brew" several cups of plain water to empty the external and any internal tanks. Fresh water makes the freshest-tasting coffee.

THE BLENDER

1 TAKE IT APART COMPLETELY. Studies show the blender gasket is one of the germiest spots in the kitchen. Why? Because most people don't know that the blender comes apart for thorough cleaning. Unscrew the blade from the jar and remove the gasket. Remove the center section from the lid, too.

2 POP IT IN THE DISHWASHER. Not all blender parts are dishwasher-safe. Check with your brand to be sure. If so, place the small parts in enclosed dishwasher baskets or secure in the top rack. The pitcher often can go in the bottom rack, or wash everything by hand in warm, soapy water. Rinse, dry, and reassemble.

3 WIPE THE BASE. With a warm, sudsy sponge, go over the base, paying special attention to any buttons or knobs. Rinse and wipe dry.

 1-MINUTE TIP! For a blender jar that's only lightly soiled, fill it halfway with water and add a few drops of dishwashing liquid. Blend for a few seconds and then rinse it thoroughly.

THE TOASTER OVEN

1 **CLEAN THE CRUMB TRAY.**
Unplug the toaster oven and remove the crumb tray. Dump any debris into the trash. Give the tray a quick wipe with a damp sponge or cloth.

2 **TACKLE THE REMOVABLE PARTS.**
Pull out the racks, pans, and, yes, even the crumb tray, and spritz them with a multipurpose cleaner. Use a nonabrasive scrubber sponge to remove any gunk. Rinse and dry.

3 **WIPE AWAY GREASE.**
Spray a regular sponge (for nonstick interiors) or a scrubber sponge with a multipurpose cleaner and wipe down the inside, outside, and glass door. Repeat on any areas with heavy buildup. Never spray the appliance or heating element directly. Rinse and let dry.

KEEP PLASTICS AWAY.

Some toaster ovens can get hot during use, so avoid placing any plastic bags or storage containers on top. Melted plastic can be difficult or impossible to remove.

EASY COOKWARE CLEANING TIPS

Some of the hardest-working pieces in your kitchen are your cooking and baking utensils. Here's how to keep them in tip-top shape.

TURN DOWN THE HEAT

Lower heat means less burned-on residue and easier cleaning. And for safety, nonstick cookware shouldn't be heated above 500°F. For high-heat cooking, like searing and browning, choose stainless steel or cast iron.

SHINE UP STAINLESS. Cleaning stainless steel takes effort, especially if food has burned on. Use a stainless steel cleanser, like **Bar Keepers Friend**® or **Cameo**® with a nonabrasive cleaning pad and a little elbow grease.

DE-GUNK GLASS. Glass bakeware may look clean when you wash it, but over time, residue builds up and becomes visible. To clean it, generously coat the bottom of the pan with baking soda and pour on some dishwashing liquid. Fill the dish with hot water and soak for 15 minutes. Clean the grime with a scrubber sponge, sprinkling on more baking soda if needed. Once dry, hold the dish up to the light, checking for traces of residue in the corners or on the handles.

DON'T DISCOUNT THE DISHWASHER. Most of today's cookware, even nonstick, is dishwasher-safe. Check your brand's care recommendations to be sure.

BE GENTLE WITH NONSTICK. The obvious benefit of nonstick cookware is that food slides off and pans are supereasy to clean with just soap and water. To keep them that way, skip the nonstick cooking spray. It bakes into the finish, making it tacky and food more likely to stick. Metal spatulas, used gently, are fine for lifting and turning, but stirring with metal spoons wears away the finish and should be avoided.

PRESERVE CAST IRON. Much of today's cast-iron cookware comes preseasoned, so that's one less step you have to do. To preserve the finish, it's best to wipe it out, then clean it by hand under hot water with a stiff brush; it's okay to use a little dishwashing detergent. Dry right away and then rub with a very light layer of cooking oil.

SOS FOR A BURNED POT

When a boiling pot boils dry, it's not a lost cause. Fill it with hot water and a generous squirt or two of dishwashing liquid. Put it back on the stove to simmer for 15 to 30 minutes, carefully loosening the burned bits with a spatula as they soften. When done, empty the pot and scrub clean.

SINK SMARTS

Second—maybe!—only to the range top and oven, the sink zone is command central in the kitchen. Restore order fast.

DECLUTTER

If possible, store only the cleaners and supplies you use in and around the kitchen in this area. Find another location for the rest. This will make room under the sink to stash dish drainers and trays when not in use so counters around the sink are clear.

ORGANIZE. Line the floor of an under-sink cabinet with inexpensive vinyl tiles or a shelf liner for easy cleaning when spills or drips happen. Use bins and door-mounted hooks or clothespins to organize and give cloths, brushes, scrubbers, and rubber gloves a place to dry after use.

HANG DISH AND HAND TOWELS. Mount decorative rods on walls or inside cabinets, or hang towels from the oven or dishwasher door handle for quicker drying and a neat look.

GO 'ROUND. A lazy Susan can corral dish detergents as well as multipurpose and metal cleaners while making them easy to access.

STASH THE TRASH. If under the sink is where you toss trash and recyclables, install dual pails mounted on smooth gliders for easy access and fewer "missed shots."

KILLING GERMS & CONTROLLING ODORS

Make your kitchen off-limits to the things that
make it stink and can make you sick.

CLEAN AND DRY THE SINK

Germs grow wherever there is water
and food, so clean the sink daily with
a bleach or germ-killing cleanser.
Pay special attention to the faucet
handles and drain. Dry the area when
you are done.

ZAP COOKING ODORS

Eliminating, not covering up, cooking
odors is key to getting rid of them for
good. Start by running your kitchen's
exhaust fan and opening the window,
even just a crack. No fan? Open the
window and simmer a mix of 2
tablespoons distilled white vinegar in 2
cups of water while you cook. When
dinner's done, spray soft surfaces, like
curtains and chair cushions, with an odor-
eliminating spray to neutralize smells
trapped in the fabrics. **Febreze Fabric**
removes lingering odors and is
safe to use on washable fabrics.

SANITIZE SPONGES

Stinky sponges are germy sponges. Toss and replace them often. The best and easiest way to de-germ them is with a five-minute soak in a mixture of 3 tablespoons chlorine bleach per quart of water. Do this weekly or whenever they have an off odor. In-between, a run through the dishwasher and the heated dry cycle will help freshen them. After every few uses, machine-launder dishcloths and dish towels in hot water with a fabric-safe bleach.

GUT GARBAGE ODORS

Keep trash contained and sprinkle baking soda liberally in the bottom of the can to absorb odors. Wash the pail often and spray it with a disinfecting spray. Flush garbage disposals and drains regularly. Baking soda that's done its job in the refrigerator can be poured into drains to absorb odors. Grind ice cubes or citrus peel slivers in the disposal to freshen.

CLEAN CUTTING BOARDS

Keep separate cutting boards for raw meat and veggies. Clean plastic boards in the dishwasher. Give wooden boards a scrub with hot sudsy water. Sanitize plastic boards with a 2-minute soak in a mix of 2 teaspoons chlorine bleach per gallon of water and air-dry. For wooden boards, up the concentration to 2 tablespoons bleach per gallon of water for the soak, then rinse with the less concentrated solution and air-dry.

 1-MINUTE TIP! Antibacterial cleaners are effective at killing germs on sink and countertop surfaces after cutting or handling raw meats, but only if you let them sit for the time (30 seconds to several minutes) specified on the label. It takes time to kill germs, so resist the urge to spray and immediately wipe.

KITCHEN CABINET UPKEEP

Treat your cabinets like fine furniture and they'll stay looking great.

HIDDEN DIRT

Vertical surfaces, like cabinet and drawer fronts, don't show grime as easily as flat surfaces do, but they attract dulling, greasy kitchen dust just the same.

HOW OFTEN TO CLEAN CABINETS

Tackle this task thoroughly once or twice yearly
with a cleaner that's safe for the material.

Laminate cabinets can be cleaned with a multipurpose cleaner. For wood cabinets, try **Parker & Bailey® Kitchen Cabinet Cream**. It safely cuts grease and leaves wood with a smooth feel and a soft glow.

Every week or so, go over and around doorknobs and drawer pulls (and wherever hands touch and grease collects) with a sudsy sponge.

 1-MINUTE TIP! Run your kitchen's exhaust fan during cooking—especially while frying or sautéing. In addition to odors, smoke and grease particles will be drawn out instead of settling on surfaces.

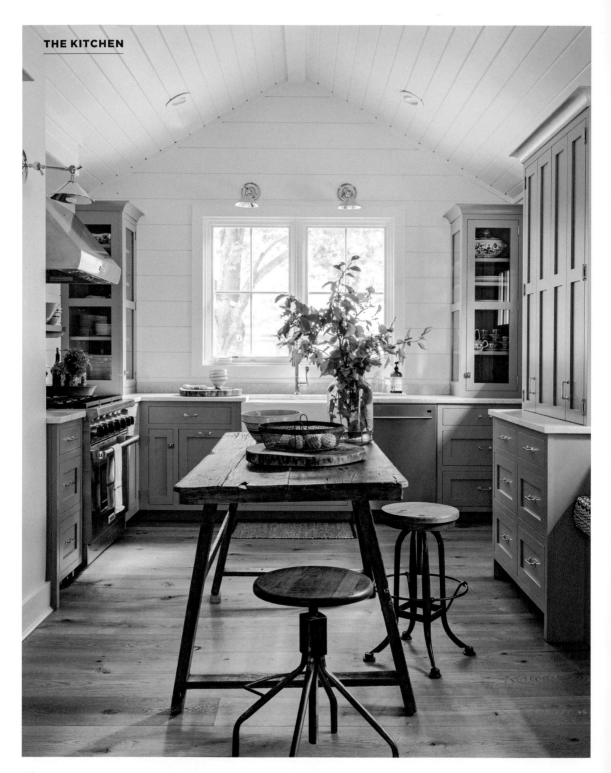

5 NO-SKIP KITCHEN FLOOR-CLEANING TIPS

1 KEEP A MINI VAC HANDY.
Stash a lightweight stick vac in a closet close to your kitchen. It's perfect for handling dry spills quickly and makes after-dinner floor cleanup a cinch.

2 NAB STICKY MESSES.
Wine dribbles or jelly blobs dry in no time and are not only hard to remove but attract more dirt. Spritz a little cleaner on a paper towel and wipe to remove stains. Dab a damp paper towel into a little baking soda to rub out scuff marks.

3 VACUUM FIRST, THEN MOP.
This way, you'll capture loose dirt and dust before it sticks to the floor and gets pushed around by the mop.

4 LAY DOWN A MAT.
Before any messy cooking projects, like frying or making pasta or pizza, place a large towel on the floor to catch any spills or grease splatters. When done, shake out and wash the towel, and admire your clean floor!

5 DON'T OVERLOOK THE NOOKS.
Dust gets caught in hard-to-reach places, like under the cabinet toe kick, around chair and table legs, and along the base of the refrigerator. Use your vacuum's hose and crevice tool to nab the dust and hair lurking there.

BISSELL CROSSWAVE® ALL-IN-ONE MULTI-SURFACE CLEANER

This unique floor-cleaning appliance both vacuums and washes bare floors and area rugs. In tests, it was easy to use and clean and a time-saver.

SMART SPIN

Today's hi-tech appliances make doing laundry so easy, your family will be clamoring to help (almost)!

chapter

3

LAUNDRY & CLOTHING CARE

"An actress once advised me, 'Make sure you do your own laundry—it will keep you honest.'"

—Cate Blanchett, actress

To some, laundry is a never-ending chore. To others, clean laundry is a satisfying accomplishment. Whichever camp you fall into, we've got you covered! In this chapter, you'll find tips to help speed the process along; ways to ensure stain-removal success; a timetable for how often items need washing or dry cleaning; tips for better ironing results, safer clothing storage, and more. Doing laundry just got a whole lot easier!

DO LAUNDRY FASTER & SMARTER

These simple tips will help streamline this important task.

PRESORT BEFORE LAUNDRY DAY

Place dual baskets or divided hampers in each bedroom so family members can help sort lights from darks as they undress. This also helps keep clothes off the floor and the room looking neater.

STOP PAIRING

Matching socks takes time when you're digging through a giant heap to find a mate. Invest in sock clips. **Sock Cop® Sock Clips** "handcuff" sock pairs together in the wash, through the dryer, and back into the drawer.

PRETREAT AHEAD OF WASHING

Make stains easier to remove by using a laundry pretreater that can be applied days before you do the laundry. Check the product label to be sure, because not all can. Apply it and then put the garment into the hamper. It will start to work before you are ready to wash. **Shout® Advanced Ultra Concentrated Gel** can be safely applied to fabrics up to one week before they're washed.

MACHINE-WASH DELICATES

Today's washers have very gentle cycles. Many items labeled as "hand wash" can be safely laundered in the machine. Place items in mesh laundry bags, select cool water, and begin the gentlest cycle your machine offers. Air-dry items unless you know they can be safely tumble-dried.

SORTING STRATEGIES

Just a few steps to keep colors bright and protect fabrics from damage.

1 START WITH COLOR.
Clothes with saturated colors and deep hues are more likely to release dye, so group them together. If you have a possible bleeder (apply a drop of water and dab with a white paper towel to check), wash it separately the first few times.

2 MOVE ON TO FABRIC.
Separate lint "givers" from lint "receivers." That means towels or fuzzy sweaters shouldn't be washed or dried with corduroy or velour. It's also best to keep fabrics of similar weights together, so coarse fabrics don't abrade and damage delicate ones and all items in the load finish drying at the same time.

3 FINISH WITH SOIL LEVEL.
Very dirty or stained laundry needs extra attention. These items can often benefit from more detergent or longer, more aggressive cycles. Sorting by the amount of soil will keep excess soil from redepositing on less-dirty items.

KNOW YOUR LAUNDRY PRODUCTS

Choosing the right formulas will give you the best results.

DETERGENTS

A good laundry detergent is essential for removing stains, washing away soil, and keeping whites and colors bright. Powders are less expensive, liquids make good stain treaters, and packs are convenient to use. Always measure powders or liquids and add more of any detergent for large or heavily soiled loads.

PRETREATERS

Formulated to remove a wide variety of stains, these sprays or gels penetrate deeply and start breaking down stains before items go in the wash. Most of these products should be applied only about 5 to 10 minutes before washing. Some can be applied up to one week before to help keep stains from setting and make them easier to remove. Double-check the label to be sure.

FABRIC SOFTENERS

Liquid fabric softeners are added to the final rinse cycle. They coat and penetrate fibers to smooth and condition them. Dryer sheets impart light softness and help control static. Avoid using them on children's sleepwear and fleece, athletic apparel, and microfiber cloths, where they reduce absorbency and flame resistance. To keep towels absorbent, don't use more fabric softener than the label recommends, and don't use it in every cycle.

BLEACHES

Chlorine and color-safe bleaches are the two types to have on hand to remove stains from whites and colors. Follow care-label recommendations on which is safe to use, or test in a hidden spot.

HOW OFTEN SHOULD YOU WASH IT?

Use this guide to help determine how frequently
most items need laundering.

EVERY WEAR
- Tights & Socks
- Blouses/Shirts
- Panties/Boxers & Briefs

EVERY 3 WEARS
- Pajamas
- Bath towels
- Bras/Camisoles
- Dresses/Skirts
- Sweaters
- Jeans/Dress pants

EVERY 1–2 DAYS
- Hand towels
- Dish towels
- Washcloths

EVERY WEEK
- Sheets
- Pillowcases
- Bathmats

EVERY 1–2 MONTHS
- Bathrobes
- Mattress pads
- Pillow liners

EVERY 3–6 MONTHS
- Shower curtains
- Throws
- Throw rugs
- Outerwear
- Comforters
- Pillows

4 STEPS TO FEWER WRINKLES

DON'T OVERLOAD the washer and dryer. Cramming items in can cause creases.

SHAKE OUT WET CLOTHES when moving them from the washer to the dryer, so they tumble more freely and wrinkles fall out.

IF YOUR DRYER HAS ONE, select the extended tumbling option, so clothes don't sit and creases don't set while waiting for you to unload the dryer.

REMOVE ITEMS PROMPTLY or while still damp, smooth them by hand, and fold or hang them immediately.

HOW OFTEN SHOULD YOU DRY-CLEAN IT?

Use this guide to help determine how often most things need dry cleaning.

WHAT IS DRY CLEANING?

In dry cleaning, clothing does get wet—just not with water. Instead, garments that would be damaged by water are washed and rinsed in a chemical solvent that cleans and removes stains. Afterward, items are dried, aired out to remove any lingering odors, and pressed. A good shop uses clean, filtered solvents, so none should remain in fabrics after cleaning. However, it is still a good idea to remove the plastic bags covering the dry-cleaned clothes once you get home, allowing clothes to breathe.

EVERY 1–2 WEARS
- Shirts
- Blouses
- Evening wear

EVERY 3 WEARS
- Sweaters
- Skirts
- Pants
- Everyday dresses
- Suits

EVERY 6 MONTHS
- Throw pillows
- Comforters
- Duvet covers
- Bedspreads

EVERY YEAR
- Curtains & Drapes

EVERY SEASON
- Outdoor Jackets & Coats

CAN I HAND-WASH IT WHEN THE LABEL SAYS "DRY CLEAN"?

Maybe. While many items labeled "Dry Clean" can be safely hand-washed, keep in mind that whenever you go against the care label, you are taking a risk. How to know? Assess the construction, color, and fabric of the garment. A soft blouse may be worth trying but not a tailored jacket. Place a drop of water on a hidden spot and blot with a paper towel. If the color bleeds, don't risk it. Some fabrics, like rayon, may shrink, and silk may lose its soft feel if it's hand-washed. And if the garment's label says "Dry Clean Only," washing by hand may ruin it. Sometimes it's the trims or embellishments on a garment that make it require dry cleaning. If you follow the care label and something still goes wrong, try returning it for a refund.

5 COMMON HAND-WASHING MISTAKES

Avoid these common errors to give your delicates and specialty items the care they deserve.

1 PUTTING GARMENTS IN FIRST. Think of hand-washing as giving your clothes a bath. Just as you don't get into an empty tub, your sweater shouldn't, either. Forceful water hitting a garment can stress it, and detergent poured directly on it can be harder to rinse out. Instead, fill the sink or basin with warm or cool water. As it's filling, add detergent and swish the water to be sure it's completely dissolved. Lay the garment in the water and press down to fully immerse it.

2 RINSING WITH THE FAUCET. Holding delicates up under running water can cause fabrics to stretch, so rinse them the same way you washed them: in a bath of clear water. Scoop up the entire garment and, if it's lightweight, like lingerie or a bathing suit, place it in a colander. With a faucet sprayer, rinse it directly in the colander. If it's not lightweight, fill the sink or basin with cool, clear water; immerse the item; and squeeze the water through it to rinse.

3 SCRUBBING STAINS. Aggressive scrubbing can damage fabrics, especially fragile ones. Treat stains by gently working laundry detergent into the stain with your fingertips. Then, as it soaks, gently squeeze sudsy water through the garment. Most items will be clean in about 15 minutes. Some heavily soiled items may need more time.

4 WRINGING OUT THE WATER.
Twisting and tightly wringing wet, delicate fabrics is a surefire way to damage them. To remove excess moisture, carefully lift the garment out of the rinse water with both hands and gently squeeze out as much as you can.

5 BLOTTING OUT MOISTURE.
Lay wet garments flat on an absorbent towel. Roll the towel and garment together, gently squeezing as you go, then unroll. If the garment is still wet, roll it in another clean, dry towel.

6 HANGING ITEMS TO DRY.
To ensure that delicates, especially knits, don't stretch out of shape, always lay them flat to dry. Lay a sweater or bathing suit on top of a dry towel or on a mesh drying rack, blocking it into shape, and allow it to air-dry. Once the front is dry, turn it over so the back can do the same.

 1-MINUTE TIP! No time to hand-wash? Place items in a mesh bag and select your machine's gentlest cycle. Some new models even have an extra-gentle hand-wash cycle. Skip the dryer, though. Reshape the item and lay it flat to dry.

HOW TO FIX
LAUNDRY MISHAPS

Sometimes, even when you follow the rules, things go wrong.
Here's help for when they do.

PROBLEM The colors from one item bled onto another.

THE FIX Try washing the stained item again by itself in warm water with detergent and color-safe bleach. Or try Good Housekeeping Lab pick **Carbona® Color Run Remover**, which safely removes transfer-dye stains from a single item or an entire load.

PROBLEM A tissue left in a pocket went through the wash.

THE FIX Before taking out the load, rewash it with a dose of fabric softener added to the final rinse. Pull off whatever you can by hand, then tumble-dry the load (the dryer's lint filter will capture most of it). Use a lint roller or a dry scrubber sponge to remove any remaining specks.

 1-MINUTE TIP! For loads with colors that you think might bleed, like jeans or brights, toss in a color-grabbing cloth like **Shout Color Catcher®** or **Carbona Dye Grabber™**. These disposable cloths pick up and hold on to small amounts of loose dye so they don't resettle onto other garments. Keep in mind, though, that these cloths usually can't prevent big disasters, like a red item that turns an entire load pink.

PROBLEM A stained item went through the dryer.

THE FIX This might be difficult to remedy—but it's not impossible. Saturate the spot with Good Housekeeping Lab Pick **Shout Advanced Gel**, working it deep into the fabric, and allow it to set overnight. Apply a bit more and launder with chlorine or color-safe bleach in the warmest water that's safe for the fabric. Repeat if necessary. Keep the item out of the dryer until you're sure the stain is completely gone.

PROBLEM Your favorite sweater has shrunk.

THE FIX Sadly, this is one oops you might have to live with. If the shrinkage is minimal, try rewetting the sweater and then carefully stretching it out and reshaping it.

HOW TO WASH PILLOWS & COMFORTERS

Cleaning down- and polyester-filled bedding is easier than you think.

USE A LARGE-CAPACITY WASHER

Front-loading or top-loading washers without agitators are best for washing bulky pillows and comforters. These machines clean gently without damage. If you don't own such a machine, consider using a laundromat.

SELECT THE CORRECT CYCLE.
Choose the Bulky Bedding cycle if your washer has one; if not, select Delicates. These cycles clean but aren't overly aggressive, so they don't destroy the shape of these items. Select a warm water temperature.

RUN AN EXTRA RINSE AND SPIN.
This extra step helps ensure that any detergent residue is removed and not trapped inside.

TUMBLE-DRY LOW.
Use a gentle heat and toss in a few dryer balls to keep pillows and comforters tumbling and prevent the filling from clumping. Stop the dryer midcycle and remove and fluff comforters and pillows two or three times to maintain loft.

 1-MINUTE TIP! In most cases, foam bedding should not be washed unless recommended on the care label. Wash removable covers and spot-clean foam, if necessary.

THE GOLDEN RULES OF STAIN REMOVAL

With these basic principles, no stain on washable fabrics will get the best of you.

TACKLE STAINS PROMPTLY.
The longer a stain sits, the more difficult it is to remove. If you can't launder a stained garment right away, spot-treat it with a little soap and water, or apply a stain remover that can sit for several days before washing to keep the stain from setting.

BLOT; DON'T RUB.
Use an absorbent cloth to gently blot stains out of fabric before applying any stain remover. Rubbing pushes a stain farther in and damages fibers.

START GENTLE, GO STRONGER.
When stains require multiple steps or products, try the gentlest method first and work up to the most aggressive, as needed.

TEST ANY METHOD IN A HIDDEN SPOT.

It's hard to predict how every fabric will respond to a stain remover, so always test any product you are using for the first time on a hidden area, like the hem or a seam, for any color fading or spotting.

PUT A PAD UNDERNEATH TO ABSORB THE STAIN.

Place a paper towel or cloth under a stain as you remove it. The pad will absorb the stain as it dissolves and keep it from spreading.

SKIP THE DRYER UNTIL THE STAIN IS GONE.

Never place an item in the dryer until you know a stain is completely removed; otherwise, it may be permanently set.

LAUNDRY ROOM UPKEEP

Don't take safety for granted; protect your family from hidden hazards.

STORE CLEANING PRODUCTS SAFELY

Detergents (especially single-use packs), bleaches, and all cleaning products should be kept well out of kids' reach during use and while in storage. It takes only seconds for little ones to grab and ingest products that can harm them.

DON'T DECANT

Resist the urge to transfer products into decorative containers. It may look pretty, but it's always safest to keep cleaning products in their original containers, which list ingredients, directions, and first-aid recommendations.

CLEAN THE WASHER

Studies show that bacteria can remain in a washing machine even at the end of a cycle. And water that puddles in dispensers and gaskets causes mold growth and musty smells. To keep your machine clean, run an empty cycle with **Tide® Washing Machine Cleaner** once a month. Regularly remove and wash dispensers and wipe gaskets dry after use. Leave the washer door open between uses to promote drying.

VACUUM THE DRYER

Lint buildup inside and around the dryer is a fire hazard. Clean your dryer's lint filter after every load. Vacuum and keep the floor under and around the dryer lint-free. Once a year, disconnect the vent and vacuum the back of the dryer and as far into each end of the vent as you can reach. Make sure any outside exhaust is free of leaves and debris.

7 IRONING MISTAKES TO AVOID

Here's how not to destroy your favorite clothes—or your iron.

BE BEST PRESSED

There's no need to fear it. Knowing how to iron correctly takes you from shabby to chic in minutes.

1 **IRONING DRY FABRICS.**
Wrinkles are easier to remove when fabrics are still damp. If you can't iron garments as you take them from the dryer, use your iron's spray feature to mist and soften the fabric before passing the iron over it. Zap extra-stubborn wrinkles with a burst of steam.

2 **SAVING DELICATES FOR LAST.**
You can make the process go more smoothly and avoid any drips or burns by ironing the most delicate fabrics first, at lower temperature settings. Then work your way up to cotton and linen.

3 **AUTOMATICALLY CRANKING UP THE HEAT.**
If a garment is made of a blend, select the setting for the more delicate fiber. It will help preserve your garment and eliminate shiny or burned spots.

4 **NOT USING TAP WATER.**
Today's irons can handle tap water better than older models could. Unless your area's water is extremely hard, there's no reason to use distilled water. For areas with very hard water, mix it 50/50 with distilled. And avoid using water that's gone through a home water-softening system that uses salt. The salt can be corrosive to the inside of the iron.

5 **USING VINEGAR TO CLEAN YOUR IRON.**
An iron's metal interior is not designed to handle an acid like distilled white vinegar, so using it can damage the working parts of your iron. Clean the inside by holding it over a sink and pumping the steam-burst feature, or as recommended by the manufacturer. Clean the soleplate of burned-on residue with a baking soda paste or with **Faultless® Hot Iron Cleaner**.

6 **STORING THE IRON WITH WATER IN IT.**
Always empty the iron's water tank and allow the last few drops to steam out before putting the iron away, especially if you store it on its soleplate. This keeps excess water from damaging the internal parts and leaking through and discoloring the soleplate.

7 **NOT LETTING SPRAY STARCH SOAK.**
To add a crisp finish, spray starch must soak in before the iron hits the fabric. If you just spray and press, you risk getting a burned, sticky residue on your iron's soleplate.

WHEN TO IRON &
WHEN TO STEAM

A clothes steamer is a quick alternative to an iron, but it can't do everything. Know what each appliance does best.

CREASE RELIEF

No steamer? No worries. Hold your iron vertically and press the burst-of-steam button to quickly freshen fabrics while they're still on the hanger.

USE AN IRON FOR

- A crisp finish, like on cotton dress shirts
- Sharp pleats and creases
- Large flat items, like tablecloths and sheets
- Heavy fabrics, like denim
- Flattening newly sewn seams and hems
- Applying decals and patches

USE A STEAMER FOR

- Soft fabrics with flowing details, like silks and chiffons
- Jackets, suits, and items that are difficult to iron flat
- Curtains and drapes while hanging on the rod
- Sequins and embellishments that ironing can damage
- Lace and embroidery to keep it from flattening
- Velvet, suede, and other napped or brushed fabrics

HOW IT WORKS: DOWNY* WRINKLE RELEASER* PLUS!

This spray completely eliminates the need to iron certain garments and makes the ironing of others much easier. Ingredients coat and relax the fibers to help creases fall out, and wrinkles disappear as the fabric dries. Just spritz, tug, and—presto! It smooths light- to medium-weight fabrics and removes odors from clothing and bedding. It's water-based formula is not recommended for dry clean–only fibers, like silk and rayon. It also comes in a mini 3-ounce bottle to de-wrinkle at the office or while traveling.

SAFE CLOTHING STORAGE

Fabrics will stay protected from one season to the next with these simple steps.

MAKE SURE EVERYTHING IS CLEAN

Launder anything you've worn—even once—or, if it's not washable, take it to the dry cleaner. Unremoved stains and soil may yellow during storage and attract insects.

FOLD, DON'T HANG, KNITS

Sweaters and other knit fabrics can stretch if hung during storage. Fold or roll them instead. If space is tight, drape the sturdiest ones over the crossbar of a hanger that you've covered with a cloth or pillowcase.

CHOOSE THE RIGHT LOCATION

A hot attic or a damp basement is not an ideal clothing storage location. If you can, try to store clothes in the main part of your home, where temperature and humidity are regulated. Fabric garment bags, storage boxes, and even hard plastic storage bins are all acceptable containers. Just remove clothes from plastic dry-cleaning bags. These thin plastic bags can break down during storage and damage fabrics.

SKIP MOTHBALLS

In most cases, if clothing is clean and stored properly, mothballs, which can leave behind a hard-to-remove odor, aren't necessary. Cedar repels young moths but not adult ones. Keep closets clean and dust free to deter moths.

ALL TUCKED IN

Strategically place baskets in unexpected
places, like this nightstand, to help corral
and hide clutter.

BEDROOMS, FAMILY ROOMS & HOME OFFICES

"I hate housework. You do the dishes, make the beds, and six months later you have to start all over again."

—*Joan Rivers, comedian*

Coming home after a stressful day is most restorative when you walk into clean, calming spaces. Whether you hope to catch up on a little TV, a little work, or a little sleep, this chapter will ensure that your bedrooms, family spaces, and home-office areas are relaxing sanctuaries. You'll find speedy tips for controlling clutter, banishing dust, and deep-cleaning mattresses, floors, window coverings, and more. Yes—there really is no place like home.

FAST FIXES FOR A SPOTLESS BEDROOM

If you tidy up daily and deep-clean weekly with these simple steps, an organized oasis will await you.

MAKE THE BED

Do this before any dusting and vacuuming so you aren't generating dust that will fall onto clean surfaces. Fluff decorative pillows.

PUT EVERYTHING AWAY

Start by stowing any clothing or shoes littering the room and taking any dirty items to the hamper. Store any loose jewelry lying around and remove books, magazines, cups, and any other items cluttering surfaces that don't belong there.

DUST WISELY

Spray a cloth with furniture polish and wipe the tops of night tables and dressers, lamps, and the wooden headboard and footboard, if you have them. Straighten up items that stay on display.

HIT THE FLOORS

Vacuum the carpet or flooring around the bed and other furniture. Start at the far corner of the room and work your way backward out the door.

MATTRESS & BEDDING CARE

A clean bed is more than just clean sheets. But relax;
deep-cleaning takes only minutes.

DITCH DUST

Use your vacuum cleaner's upholstery
tool to go over the top and sides of the
mattress and as much of the foundation as
you can. Press firmly on the tool to draw
out dust beneath the fabric's surface.
Use the crevice tool to get into the
quilting, edge welting, and where any
pillow top is attached.

ZAP STAINS

Remove pet or food stains with a carpet
cleaner like Good Housekeeping Lab
pick **Bissell Professional Pet Stain and
Odor Remover.** It removes both stains
and odors from mattress coverings, and
because it's formulated for carpeting, it is
easy to rinse out. Avoid overwetting the
mattress, and let it dry completely
before making the bed.

KILL ODORS

Freshen your mattress by sprinkling baking soda onto the fabric to absorb odors. Work it into the fabric with your hand or a soft brush. Wait 15 minutes, then vacuum. Sanitize with a disinfecting spray, like **Lysol**. It's safe to use on fabrics and kills bacteria that cause odors.

DEEP-CLEANING

If you have a garment or household steamer, go over the mattress with it to help kill dust mites lurking near the surface. Then vacuum them away.

PILLOW TALK

Washing is just the beginning. Here's what to know
to keep pillows up to "fluff."

WHEN TO REPLACE THEM

How do you know when it's time to toss
a pillow? Fold it in half and place a heavy
book on top for 30 minutes—if it doesn't
spring back into shape once the book is
removed, it's time for a new one.

"DUST" WITH THE DRYER.

Between cleanings, tumble pillows (even foam) in the dryer on the no-heat or air-only cycle for 10 to 15 minutes to remove dust and help fluff them.

PICK THE PROPER PILLOW.

When you are in the market for a new pillow, choose one based on your preferred sleep position. Side sleepers need a thick, firm one; stomach snoozers a thin, soft one; and back sleepers somewhere in between. What's key is keeping your neck and spine aligned. Choose down, synthetic, foam, or combination fillings based on what feels best to you.

PROTECT AGAINST ALLERGENS.

Encase pillows (and mattresses) in coverings that are barriers against dust, mites, and other sniffle-inducing particles for easy breathing.

GH Seal–holder Protect-A-Bed® encasements keep bedding clean and allergens away and can be washed in hot water without shrinking.

3 THINGS YOU CAN DO WITH A PILLOWCASE

PROTECT CLOTHES

Fashion an instant garment bag by cutting a small slit in the closed end of the case and slipping a hanger through.

WASH TOYS

Drop washable plush toys inside and knot the case before placing it in the washer. The toy will get clean and stay protected. Wash on a gentle cycle and select a double rinse to remove all traces of detergent.

STOW SHEETS

Stash a folded set of sheets inside one of the pillowcases to keep your linen closet neat and organized and make the set easy to remove from the shelf.

HOW TO NEATLY FOLD
A FITTED SHEET

It's easier than you think, even without a helper.
Just follow these four simple steps.

GET A NEATER LINEN CLOSET

Once you master this technique,
your sheets will be easier to store and
your linen closet will go from mess
to marvelous!

1 **TURN THE SHEET INSIDE-OUT.**
With the elastic facing you, place your hands into two adjacent corners.

3 **REPEAT STEP 2 WITH THE OTHER TWO CORNERS.** When you're done, the sheet will be folded in half horizontally with two sets of double corners. The top side of the sheet is now facing out.

2 **FLIP ONE CORNER OVER THE OTHER.** Invert the corner in your right hand over the corner in your left so the left corner is tucked inside the right.

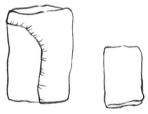

4 **FOLD VERTICALLY.** Invert one set of corners over the other so all corners are tucked into one (the elastic should form a semicircle). Lay it flat and smooth. Fold in thirds lengthwise, then in thirds again.

 1-MINUTE TIP! Steal a home-stager secret and make the bed with the top sheet facedown so the finished side is up once the bed is made. If you have the time, go one step further: Iron the pillowcases and use a steamer on the section of top sheet that is visible.

FRESHEN UP THE GUESTROOM FAST

Get ready for overnight guests—even last-minute ones—in no time.

REFRESH THE BED

Make up the bed with fresh sheets, and check that blankets and coverings are appropriate for the season. Fluff the pillows in your dryer on the Air-Only cycle for 10 minutes. Spritz sheets with a softly scented linen spray for a relaxing touch.

CLEAR CLOSET SPACE

Take 10 hangers' worth of clothes from the middle of the closet and relocate them to another room. Add fresh hangers to the cleared space.

BANISH DUST

Turn on the lights and open the blinds so you can spot even the most hidden dust. Check light-fixture globes for bugs and spider webs. Unscrew them to remove, wash, and replace. With a cloth, go over furniture, lamps, headboard, mirrors, windowsills, and picture frames. Empty the wastebasket, and vacuum around the furniture and bed.

ADD A LUGGAGE RACK

Skip emptying drawers. Instead, pick up an inexpensive luggage rack so guests can access clothing right out of their bags. But do declutter the nightstand and set out a pretty dish to hold jewelry and loose change.

RELOCATE FRAGILE KEEPSAKES

Remove delicate treasures to lower stress for you and your guests. Replace them with a water carafe and glasses, extra toiletries, or helpful information, like local maps and brochures.

CLEAN UP KIDS' CHAOS

Start by corraling kids' clutter so their rooms are easier to clean.

CLEAR POCKETS

Recycle a plastic over-the-door shoe pocket organizer as easy-to-reach containers for small toys, from baby rattles to doll accessories. Hang them within reach of each of your children to encourage them to put their toys away.

CATCHALL HAMPERS

Woven fabric or wicker laundry bins are great toy keepers for bigger kids who can reach down to the bottom. Hang a mesh toy hammock in the corner of the room as a catchall for plush toys.

SHARED-ROOM STORAGE

Pullout bins are great for rooms with multiple kids. Designate low ones for the youngest and label them with colored tags or pictures of the contents so that putting items back is easy for all.

EASY ACCESS

Open shelves are ideal for holding board games and puzzles and displaying "collections" and awards. Use an extendable tool, like Good Housekeeping Lab pick **Swiffer 360° Duster**, to keep shelves and their contents clean and dust-free.

CLUTTER SOLUTIONS

Try these ideas to make sure your living and family rooms stay mess-free.

DARE TO BE SPARE

Ease congestion in these rooms by sticking to the basics when it comes to furniture—a sofa, comfy chairs, and a coffee table. If you have room, add a side table. Arrange the pieces for clear, unimpeded traffic flow.

TABLE THAT

Corral small items, like candles and vases, on a tray (so they're easy to move when company's coming). Store TV remotes in a lidded basket on a lower shelf.

DOUBLE UP

Maximize storage and get extra seating with a hide-stuff-inside ottoman. Pare throw pillows down to a few in complementary patterns and colors.

SPEED-CLEAN IN MINUTES

All you need is a quick sweep of family spaces to get them in shape fast.

PURGE PAPERWORK

Gather newspapers, books, magazines, and electronic devices. Stack them neatly in baskets or stash them in racks or on shelves. Remove items like shoes and toys that don't belong there.

GO OVER UPHOLSTERY

Stash a sticky lint roller in a nearby drawer and use it to quickly grab lint and pet hair from chair cushions and backs.

CLEAR AWAY DUST

Use a microfiber cloth or duster to go over flat surfaces where dust is most noticeable—coffee table, end tables, TV screen, and lamp bases. Leave the hidden spots for another day.

VACUUM THE FLOOR

With a lightweight, easy-to-grab stick vac, clean surface litter and lint from the center of the room, paying special attention to the areas around the sofa and side chairs.

3 WAYS TO SPIFF UP WOOD FLOORS

Bring back the glow with barely any effort.

1 RUB OUT SCUFFS. Rub light marks with the sock on your foot (no bending required) or a clean tennis ball. For more stubborn marks, apply baking soda to a damp cloth and gently rub the scuff until it disappears. Wipe with a clean, damp cloth and buff dry.

2 CLEAR THE WAY. Remove dirt from traffic lanes and in front of chairs with a cleaner formulated for wood, like Good Housekeeping Lab pick **Weiman Hardwood Floor Cleaner**. Lightly spritz a 3-foot-square area with the cleaner, then go over it with a damp microfiber mop or cloth; let dry. Rinse the cloth or mop often.

3 SHOO AWAY GOO. To pry off tacky messes, like tar or candle wax, place a few ice cubes in a plastic bag and hold it against the blob to harden it. Gently scrape it off with a plastic spatula or credit card. Coax off dried paint splatters by holding a cloth dipped in rubbing alcohol on the drip for a few seconds. Use a baking soda paste to finish the job. Rinse and dry.

3 MISTAKES THAT CAN RUIN WOOD FLOORS

Avoid these common cleaning blunders
to keep your floors looking their best.

1 VACUUMING WITH A ROTATING BRUSH. To keep from scratching and marring your floor's finish, use a canister vacuum's floor brush attachment or switch off the spinning brush on an upright vacuum.

2 WET-CLEANING TOO OFTEN. Newer floor finishes are more resistant to water, but it's always best to tackle small areas at a time with a damp (not wet) mop or cloth and dry them promptly. Wet-clean wood floors only as needed.

3 OVERUSING STEAM. Steam mops clean without chemicals, but use them sparingly, if at all, on wood. Choose the lightest level of steam and don't linger on one spot for too long. Never use steam on waxed or worn wood floors.

SO LONG, CARPET STAINS!

Yes, you can get rid of them once and for all! (And see our complete stain removal guide in Chapter 7, page 148.)

DON'T RUB IT IN

If you attack a stain vigorously, you'll only untwist the carpet tufts. Instead, blot gently and work from the stain's outer edge toward the center.

DON'T SPRAY THE CARPET

Applying too much cleaner only makes it harder to rinse out and leaves a residue that attracts dirt. Spray the cloth you're using and dab the stain instead.

RINSE SPARINGLY

Never pour water directly on a carpet. It will saturate the padding and flooring underneath and damage them. Instead, dip a cloth in clear water and dab the carpet to rinse. Blot with a dry cloth.

STOP STUBBORN STAINS

Residue deep in the carpet may travel up the fibers as they dry and resurface as a stain. To prevent this, place paper towels and a heavy pot or vase on top and leave overnight. In the morning, fluff to dry.

DEEP-CLEANING OPTIONS

Choose one of these ways to keep carpets looking great.

BUY

If you have the room to store it, buying a carpet deep-cleaning machine means that you can tackle stains and traffic paths regularly. And your purchase cost will likely be repaid with just a few uses. **Bissell Proheat 2x Revolution Pet Pro Carpet Cleaner** is easy to maneuver and has an Express Mode for quicker cleaning and faster drying.

RENT

When you rent, you don't need storage space, but you do have to pick the machine up and return it to the store. Choose a retailer with machines that are clean and well-maintained. Always try out the vacuum on a scrap piece of carpet or a mat before using it on your carpet to be sure it works well.

PRO

Likely the most expensive but also the most convenient way to go, professional carpet cleaners have equipment more powerful and effective at removing embedded dirt than home machines. Before hiring any company, get recommendations from friends and neighbors, and ask companies for an estimate, whether the technicians move furniture and apply stain-preventive treatments, and about any warranty.

DON'T MAKE THESE 4 DUSTING MISTAKES

Here's what not to do to give
your furniture the care it deserves.

USING A FEATHER DUSTER

This tool simply spreads dust from one surface to another. Instead, use a microfiber or electrostatic duster, like **Swiffer 360° Dusters**™, to grab and hold on to dust. Use a long-handled version for the tops of bookcases and ceiling fans. Wash or replace the duster when it gets dirty.

NEGLECTING HEATING AND AIR-CONDITIONING VENTS

These grilles on your walls and ceilings are dust magnets. To keep dust from blowing back into your room, go over the slats with your vacuum's soft brush attachment.

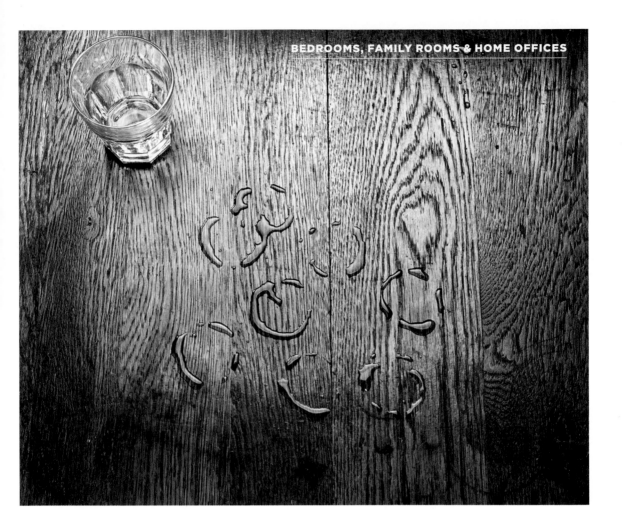

DRY DUSTING Dust particles are abrasive and, when wiped dry, may put fine scratches in your furniture's finish. Dry dust is also harder to collect. Spritz microfiber dusters and cloths with a dusting spray or polish for easier cleaning and better results.

SPRAYING POLISH ON FURNITURE Do this and you risk forming a filmy buildup on your wood that is difficult to remove and attracts more dust. Spray your cloth instead and pass it gently across the surface. Buff any excess with a clean cloth.

 1-MINUTE TIP! If you place a drippy glass or a hot dish directly on a wood table, moisture will become trapped in the finish, leaving a white ring or mark. To remove that mark, place a thick towel on the blemish and press for a few seconds with a warm, dry iron. Repeat until the ring disappears. Polish and buff well.

HOW TO FRESHEN UP WINDOW COVERINGS

Clean windows are only part of the equation.
Blinds and shades need care, too.

ALUMINUM AND VINYL BLINDS

Lower the blind and tilt the slats partially closed. Hold the bottom rail and vacuum the blind horizontally or top to bottom with your vacuum's soft dusting brush. Dampen a microfiber cloth and wipe the slats again. Open and allow them to air-dry. Good Housekeeping Lab pick **Casabella Microfiber Blind Gloves** can be used wet or dry and on either hand to quickly and easily clean dusty blinds.

VINYL AND FABRIC SHADES

Vacuum fabric shades with a dusting or upholstery tool. Clean vinyl shades with a sudsy cloth, starting at the bottom. Rinse with another cloth. Work your way up the shade to the roller. Leave it fully extended to dry.

CURTAINS AND DRAPES

Washable curtains and drapes should be laundered according to the manufacturer's care instructions. Hang them promptly to keep creases from setting. Skip ironing. Instead, smooth them with a garment steamer while they are hanging on the rod.

 1-MINUTE TIP! Spray fabric shades, curtains, and draperies with an antistatic product, like **Static Guard**, to help repel dust and pet hair and make them easier to clean.

HOW TO KEEP A CLEAN DESK & OFFICE

Make this space one you'll want to work in.

MAXIMIZE YOUR SPACE.
Mount a shelf to keep supplies and tools within reach but off your desk. Use baskets or magazine files to corral catalogs and other publications. Recycle old issues when new ones arrive. A rolling file cabinet can hold important papers and serve as an additional work surface. Leave only the essentials on your desk.

SHRED IT.
A supereasy thing you can do to protect yourself from identity theft is to invest in a micro-cut shredder. **Fellowes® Powershred® 99 MS Micro-Cut** handles fifteen sheets at once, along with credit cards and staples. Shred unwanted mail daily to keep it from piling up.

BE A LABELER.
Whatever your system, be sure containers, files, and boxes are clearly labeled with their contents. This will make it easier to sort, stash, and retrieve items and keep you from digging around unnecessarily.

TACK IT UP.
Install cork tiles, a bulletin board, or a magnetic photo strip to hold small notes, business cards, slips of paper, and other reminders you refer to often so they don't fall "out of sight, out of mind" or become lost or misplaced.

CLEAN SCREENS.
Electronic devices, especially smartphones, tablets, and those with touch screens, are dust and dirt magnets. Stash microfiber cloths and screen-cleaning sprays or wipes in your desk drawer, purse, or where you charge your portable devices. Clean them at least every one to two days. Always spray the cloth, not the device. For televisions, use only a dry, soft, lint-free cloth or duster or compressed air to blow away dust. Always follow the manufacturer's cleaning instructions to keep from voiding the warranty.

DE-GUNK KEYBOARDS AND REMOTE CONTROLS.
The nooks and crannies of these touchpads get pretty grimy. Gently tap keyboards upside down on the desk to dislodge dirt and food crumbs, or vacuum them with the vacuum's soft brush attachment. To remove grime, always follow the manufacturer's instructions. If you use a premoistened disinfecting or electronics wipe to remove stuck-on dirt, just be sure not to let any liquid seep inside.

WEED OUT CLUNKERS.
Nonworking or unwanted devices along with their cords and chargers take up valuable office real estate. Turn them in on your town's electronics recycling days, use store take-back programs, or check earth911.com for area e-cyclers.

ORGANIZE YOUR DESKTOP.
Going digital is a great way to eliminate a paper mess, but clutter on a computer desktop can actually slow down performance, so don't save unneeded files there. Take a second to put them into a labeled hard drive folder or in the cloud, where you'll be able to easily find them.

COUNTER CULTURE

A farmhouse dresser-turned-vanity
brings a pretty and practical vibe to
this bathroom.

THE BATHROOM

*"My idea of housework is to sweep the
room with a glance."*

—Erma Bombeck, columnist

Your bathroom is the one room in your home where you are pretty much guaranteed some alone time. Whether it's just a quick visit or an hour-long soak with a good book and a glass of wine, this space needs to be a place you want to visit. In the upcoming pages, our expert advice and surefire tips will encourage you to clean it quickly, inspire you to organize efficiently, and, most importantly, help keep it a healthy place for you and your family.

GET A CLEAN BATHROOM IN MINUTES

Make this space sparkle when company is on the way.
You know they'll go in.

GET SET UP

Grab a plastic bag to toss in any used cleaning wipes and the trash from the wastebasket. Next, pour one cup bleach into the toilet and brush the sides and under the rim. Let it sit for 5 minutes.

ZERO IN ON THE OBVIOUS

With a disinfecting wipe or a paper towel spritzed with equal parts distilled white vinegar and water, wipe away soap drips and toothpaste splatters on the sink, faucet, and countertop. If you have shower doors, give them a once-over with a fresh wipe to remove spots.

GO BACK TO THE BOWL

Run a wipe across the top and sides of the toilet tank and give the flush handle a swipe. With a clean wipe, go over, under, and around the seat and the lid. Flush the bleach that's been sitting in the bowl. Toss the used wipes into your trash bag and move on.

MAKE IT GLEAM

Wipe a bit of rubbing alcohol on your mirrors, faucets, and other bathroom fixtures with a paper towel to make chrome shine. Wipe mirrors with a damp microfiber cloth to clean and zap streaks at the same time.

SHAKE OUT THE RUG

Fluff it up so it looks recently vacuumed. With a damp paper towel, gather obvious clumps of hair and dust. Pay special attention to the corners of the room where it collects. Toss everything in the plastic bag and take it with you when you leave.

LEAVE A FRESH SCENT

Straighten the towels and just replace any dirty ones. If you have linen spray that you use to scent sheets and bedding, mist the towels lightly to give them a pretty scent. A light spritz of perfume does the trick, too.

ULTRA SPEED-CLEANING

Here's what you can do if you have almost no time to clean.

IN 2 SECONDS
Wipe away toothpaste globs with a tissue so they don't harden and make for more work later.

IN 5 SECONDS
Stretch out the shower curtain after a shower to help it dry faster and keep mildew away.

IN 30 SECONDS
Put out fresh towels—especially hand towels. Clean towels give the entire bathroom a lift.

 1-MINUTE TIP! Stubborn hard-water rings can make porcelain tubs and toilets look dirty even after you've cleaned them. Erase these deposits fast with a cleaning "stone," like Good Housekeeping Lab pick **Clorox® Toilet and Bath Cleaning Stone**. Made of recycled glass, it quickly rubs out these marks without damage. Deep rust stains need a treatment with a rust remover, like Good Housekeeping Lab pick **Bar Keepers Friend Soft Cleanser**. Apply, let sit one minute, and rinse.

KEEP YOUR BATHROOM CLEANER LONGER

A few extra steps now mean you'll have to clean less often. So worth it!

SQUEEGEE YOUR SHOWER

This tip is so important that it bears repeating. Hang a squeegee from the showerhead to wipe down the walls, tub, and shower doors. Just several minutes of work daily can really minimize total cleaning time in the long run.

STASH A CANISTER OF CLEANING WIPES

With them, you can quickly wipe up toothpaste splatters, watermarks, and other messes when you see them, so they won't have a chance to dry and become tougher to remove.

COMBAT CURTAIN BUILDUP

Spritz the bottom of a vinyl shower-curtain liner several times a month with a bleach-containing, all-purpose, or bathroom cleaner to keep soap scum, water minerals, and mildew at bay. Just let the shower rinse it off (before you step in) and you won't need to launder the curtain as often.

CREATE ORDER

A clutter-free counter instantly makes a bathroom look and feel cleaner. Discard packaging of cosmetics and toiletries and stash these personal-care items, along with hair-styling tools, in your vanity and medicine cabinet. For any you must leave out, display them in pretty jars and baskets.

INSTALL AMPLE TOWEL BARS

Towels can be messy. Your bathroom will look tidier when you hang them neatly where air can circulate. No wall space? Consider an over-the-door towel bar.

USE A WATER REPELLENT

Coat shower walls and doors with a product like **EnduroShield® Home Glass Treatment** or **Rain-X® Shower Door Water Repellent**. They help water, minerals, and soap scum bead up and run off, so there's less for you to scrub away.

SKIP BAR SOAP

Use liquid or foaming soap with a pump or even a hands-free soap dispenser instead. Eliminating the goopy soap dish will help your sink and countertop stay cleaner longer.

REUSE DRYER SHEETS

Keep a few used sheets handy to easily nab hair and dust bunnies from the floor without dragging out the vacuum cleaner or wetting a paper towel. You'll have to deep-clean less often, and your bathroom will look clean for unexpected guests (and for you, too!).

 1-MINUTE TIP! Use a continuous bowl cleaner, like Good Housekeeping Lab pick **Scrubbing Bubbles® Toilet Cleaning Gel**. Dispense a dab of gel from the syringelike wand, and the bowl gets cleaned with every flush. One application lasts up to seven days.

OOPS! 6 BATHROOM MISTAKES TO AVOID

Guard against these bathroom mishaps to up your game against germs.

1 YOU FLUSH THE TOILET WITH THE LID UP.

Leave the lid up when you flush the toilet and you almost certainly risk germy water particles spraying across the room and settling on surfaces. Make sure everyone in the household is onboard with the lid-down policy.

2 YOU STORE YOUR TOOTHBRUSH IN THE MEDICINE CABINET.

Trapped in a cabinet or a lidded container, your brush may not be able to dry between uses, creating a welcome environment for bacteria. Store brushes in an upright position, not touching each other. This is another good reason to remember to shut the toilet lid when you flush!

3 YOU LEAVE MAKEUP AND BRUSHES ON THE COUNTER.

Leaving these items out in a humid bathroom can make them susceptible to bacteria growth and place them in the path of airborne toilet germs. Store cosmetics in drawers and boxes in a separate nonhumid room. Clean brushes and replace makeup regularly.

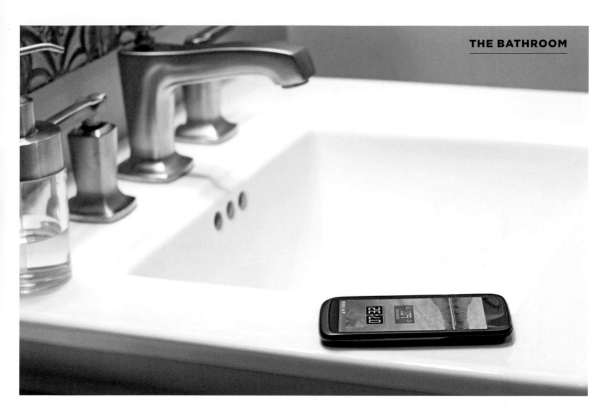

4 **YOU USE YOUR LOOFAH OR POUF FOR WAY TOO LONG.**
These shower staples, designed to hold soap and water to help you lather up, can be breeding grounds for bacteria. Rinse well after each use and hang to dry. Toss them every three to four weeks. Plastic shower poufs can be cleaned with bleach and water or in the dishwasher. Allow washcloths to dry thoroughly between uses and change them after every couple of uses or after every use if you use them to wash your face.

5 **YOU NEVER RUN THE FAN.**
Bathroom moisture can cause a host of icky issues. So run the fan or open the window (or do both!) while you shower. Keep it running for 15 to 20 minutes afterward. Regularly vacuum the fan's grille to remove dust that collects there. Most grilles can also be removed for cleaning in warm sudsy water.

6 **YOU USE YOUR CELL PHONE IN THE BATHROOM.**
Checking social media or texting while in the bathroom exposes your phone to lingering germs. And while you wash your hands, you may not clean your phone. Studies show that cell phones not only have higher bacteria counts than bathroom surfaces but also have more types of bacteria on them, too. Take a break and leave your phone out of the bathroom when you go in. Also, remember to clean it often.

BATHROOM ORGANIZERS THAT MAKE CLEANING EASIER

Maximize storage and corral clutter with these smart organizing strategies.

USE CLEAR CONTAINERS

Herd together small, oddly shaped toiletries in transparent, lidded acrylic canisters and end the mystery of where things are stashed once and for all.

PUT UP SHELVES

Compact hanging shelves and caddies turn dead wall spaces into smart storage spots.

ADD DRAWERS UNDER THE SINK

Smooth-gliding, steel-mesh drawers restore order and accessibility to a vanity without drawers. Label each one so you know what's in it and where everything should be returned.

GET A DOOR CADDY

The backs of bathroom doors are blank canvases. Use a vanity door to hang an organizer for hair-styling tools and the bathroom door for extra towels.

PUT A STOP TO MOLD & MILDEW

These seven simple steps will send these bathroom menaces packing.

1 **CHOOSE RODS OVER RINGS.**
Heavy towels dry faster when spread out to dry on a rod. Hooks and rings look pretty, but moisture can stay trapped in the folds. And when they take long to dry, mold can take hold.

2 **STRETCH THE CURTAIN.**
After every shower, spread out the shower curtain to allow water droplets to dry.

3 GET IT BEFORE IT SPREADS.

If you see a few spots of mildew along the tub's edge but don't have time for an in-depth scrub, saturate a cotton ball with bleach and place it against the stain. Continue to wet it as it dries out. It will keep the mildew from growing until you can commit to a thorough cleaning job.

4 PICK UP MATS.

Post bathing, pull up vinyl tub mats, roll loosely, and stand them up in the tub to dry. After use, drape bathmats over the edge of the tub or shower rod, or hang them in your laundry room to dry.

5 CLEAN MILDEW FROM PAINT.
Remove the shower curtain, towels, and any fabrics that could be damaged by bleach splatters. Don rubber gloves and goggles and scrub the stains with a brush and a mix of one cup chlorine bleach in one gallon warm water (test first in a hidden spot for discoloration). Let sit for 10 minutes. Rinse with a well-wrung cloth. When repainting, choose a paint that's mildew-resistant.

6 WASH THE VINYL SHOWER CURTAIN.
You know fabric shower curtains are washable, but did you know that vinyl ones are, too? Instead of tossing them when mildew strikes, launder them in hot water, with bleach, on your machine's gentle cycle. Put them in the dryer on low heat for up to 5 minutes, just to remove the excess moisture. Remove them from the dryer and rehang them to finish drying.

7 CLEAN BATH TOYS.
Children's bath toys can be breeding grounds for mold, especially when water gets trapped inside. In the bath, use solid plastic toys without holes in the bottom. Allow toys to dry thoroughly after each use and clean them regularly. If you see or suspect that they harbor mold, toss them.

TOWEL TACTICS

What's a bathroom without soft, fluffy towels? Here's what you need to know to buy the best and care for them properly.

TOWEL-BUYING TIPS

PICK COTTON. Buy 100 percent combed or ring-spun cotton—its fibers are smoothed and very tightly twisted for maximum absorbency and durability.

INSPECT THE SIDE SEAMS. Neatly folded edges (secured with close, even double stitching) signal quality. Woven edges are more likely to fray.

LOOK AT THE LOOPS. High-quality towels have tightly packed loops; the denser they are, the more absorbent the towel. Brush the loops aside—can you see the backing? If so, it's a cheapie. Pass on it.

TOWEL-CARE TIPS

SHAKE THEM OUT BEFORE DRYING. Giving towels (and all clothing) a shake before putting them in the dryer helps fluff the pile and allows them to dry more evenly.

DON'T OVERDO THE SOFTENER. A little fabric softener to impart softness and a light scent is fine, but because it coats the fibers, adding too much can hamper a towel's ability to absorb moisture. If you are a regular softener user, skip it every third or fourth load.

RESTORE THE FLUFF. If towels are scratchy, you may have a buildup of softener and hard-water minerals. Wash them without detergent, adding one cup water conditioner, like **Calgon***, and one-half cup clear ammonia instead. For smelly towels, wash with one cup distilled white vinegar, then rewash as usual.

MEDICINE CABINET MAKEOVER

Organize this compact space, and it will be easier to keep clean.

MOVE THE MEDS

Relocate medications, including herbal remedies, to a cooler, less humid location. If you have kids, use a childproof lockbox for storage.

GROUP LIKE ITEMS TOGETHER

Keep all nail-care items (files, clippers, polish) together. Do the same with eye-care items, shaving supplies, toothbrushes and other dental-care products, and more.

GO MINI

Keep small bottles and containers to hold mouthwash, cotton swabs, and more that you refill from economy sizes stored elsewhere.

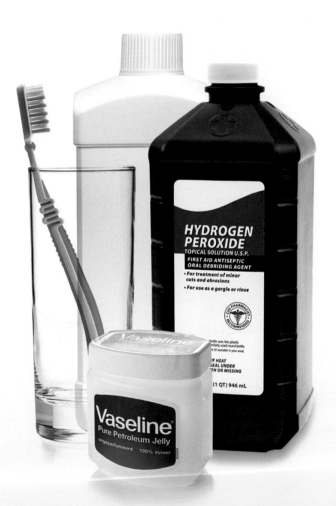

MEDICINE CABINET CLEANERS

Use these pharmacy staples for more than just bumps and bruises.

RUBBING ALCOHOL can be used to remove ballpoint pen stains from washable fabrics, shine up chrome, and remove paint splatters from floors.

HYDROGEN PEROXIDE removes bloodstains and acts like a color-safe "bleach" to lighten food stains, like wine and coffee, even on washable delicates like silk and wool. Moisten a cotton swab with the peroxide and dab it on a hidden spot to test for safety. If there's no change to the fabric, apply it to the stain.

PETROLEUM JELLY shines up and removes scuffs from patent leather and softens hard stains, like tar, so they are easier to remove.

CLEAN OUT THE LINEN CLOSET

Turn this clutter hot spot into an oasis of order.

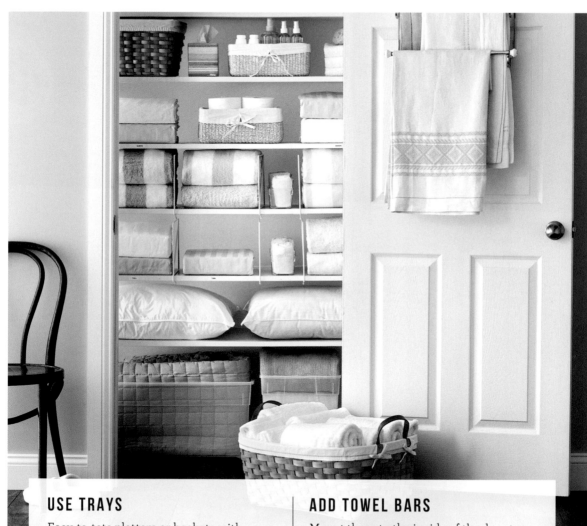

USE TRAYS

Easy-to-tote platters or baskets with handles allow amenities to move gracefully from the linen closet to the bathroom. Under-shelf bins can store extra pillowcases and washcloths.

ADD TOWEL BARS

Mount these to the inside of the door to store special occasion tablecloths, extra quilts or throws, or beach or guest towels that you might need in a hurry. This keeps you from having to riffle through the linen closet to find what you need.

ROLL TOWELS

Doing so saves you from toppling an entire stack when you need one. Rolled towels are also easier to grab.

FIGHT STALE SMELLS

Just like in the fridge, an open box of baking soda placed near your sheets and towels can prevent musty smells. Or make your own sachet by placing a new fabric softener sheet inside an envelope. Tuck it onto one of the shelves.

OUT AND ABOUT

A welcoming home starts from the outside. Look at yours from the street to assess the curb appeal others see.

THE GARAGE & OUTDOOR SPACES

"A perfect summer day is when the sun is shining, the breeze is blowing, the birds are singing, and the lawn mower is broken."

—*James Dent, humorist*

Just as you care for the interior of your home, the exterior needs attention, too—though, thankfully, not as often. In the pages to come, you'll find speedy tips for cleaning up the garage, patio, deck, and even the car. With spring comes window and gutter cleaning, and let's not forget the grill. There are simple ways to tackle these seasonal chores, too, and when these important areas are clean and organized, your home becomes more functional, more enjoyable, and a place you want to share with family and friends.

FAST FIXES FOR A CLEAN & TIDY GARAGE

Don't let this "room" become a dumping ground for out-of-season and unwanted stuff.

TRASH YOUR TRASH

Open two heavy-duty garbage bags. Into the first one, toss anything broken, empty, or rusty that can be picked up in this week's collection. Use the other bag to remove items that belong in the house or outside.

ADD WALL HOOKS

Free up floor space by adding customizable hangers and bins for tools, lawn chairs, and more. Measure your longest broom or shovel so that you mount the hooks at the correct height. **Gladiator® GearTrack®** and **GearWall®** products are easy to install individually or as part of a wall-mounted system.

ORGANIZE IN BINS

No need for fancy containers. Use flowerpots and planters for pruners, trowels, and gardening gloves. Empty garbage cans can be used for hockey sticks, baseball bats, and other long-handled items. A laundry basket makes a great catchall for soccer balls and bike helmets.

COLLECT SHOES AND BOOTS

Bring unneeded ones back in the house where they belong. Place a doormat and boot tray on the garage side of the door for clean ones that you already have and want to keep there.

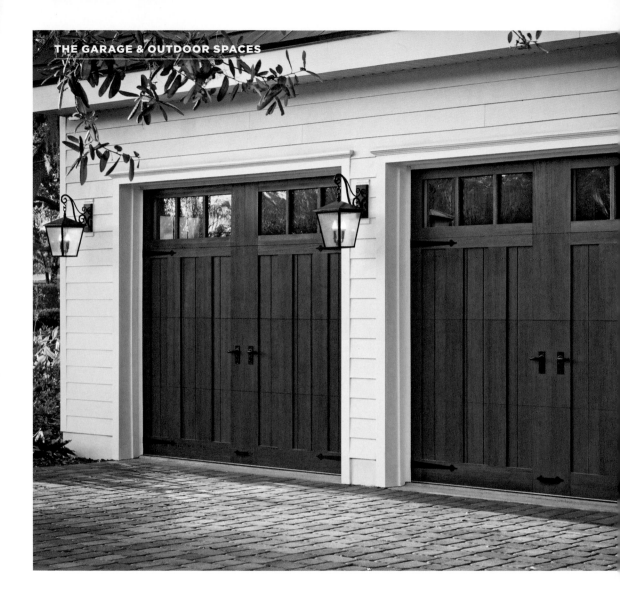

GET RID OF OIL STAINS

Sprinkle clean kitty litter on fresh stains, let it sit a few hours, and sweep away. For dried stains, sprinkle baking soda on the spot and add water to make a paste. Let sit overnight, scrub with a stiff brush, and rinse. This works for stains on the driveway, too!

SWEEP IT OUT

Grab a broom and sweep away spider webs and bugs clinging to light fixtures and around the garage door opening, steps, and the door into the house. **Clopay® Garage Doors** come in a wide array of designs and with features to perfectly match your home's needs, like added insulation or reinforcements against wind.

7 THINGS TO TAKE OUT OF THE GARAGE

Play it safe. Store these items elsewhere.

1 **LEFTOVER PAINT** won't last long if subjected to big fluctuations in temperature.

2 **CANNED FOODS** have a shorter shelf life in rooms that get hotter than 70°F. Move these goods to an indoor pantry.

3 **AN OLD REFRIGERATOR** in this uninsulated space will have to work harder in the summer and use more energy.

4 **PILES OF PAPER PLATES OR CUPS** can attract mice, which love to make nests in them.

5 **OUTDATED ELECTRONICS** should be donated or properly disposed of.

6 **OUT-OF-SEASON CLOTHING** The temperature and humidity extremes in an unsealed, unair-conditioned garage make it an unsafe space to store clothing. To keep it bug- and damage-free, it's best to store clothing in the main part of your home.

7 **PROPANE TANKS** need to be in a well-ventilated area, preferably outside.

THE BEST WAY TO STORE DANGEROUS GOODS

Keep toxic solvents, cleaners, and chemicals in a well-ventilated, lockable cabinet to protect against prying hands and careless spills. Put a clipboard inside with an ever-sharp pencil attached to keep a record of the contents and how long you've had each product.

KEEP YOUR GARAGE
CLEAN & CLUTTER-FREE

These simple ideas will reclaim this space and help you manage the mess.

PUT UP SOME PEGBOARD

A securely mounted pegboard will get your tools off the floor and out of the way. Keep a ladder or step stool handy to safely access overhead gear.

HANG SHELVES

Wooden shelves or easily installed rack units are ideal for holding seasonal items, like holiday décor or outdoor gear. Label and rotate boxes and bins on the shelves as needed.

KEEP IT IN PLAIN SIGHT

A magnetic knife strip is perfect for holding small metal tools, nails, and screws. Stow rags and other bulky items in transparent bins or wire baskets.

CREATE DESIGNATED AREAS FOR RECYCLING

The handiest spot is right next to the door leading into the garage from the house, provided the area is large enough. Choose containers with capacities greater than you normally need so that if you miss a pickup day, you won't wind up with an overflowing mound of clutter.

PATIO, PORCH & DECK SPRUCE-UPS

A good spring cleaning will set the stage for a summer of fun.

FURNITURE

Add dishwashing liquid to a bucket of warm water. With a plastic brush, gently scrub outdoor tables and chairs. To whiten dingy plastic furniture, use an all-purpose cleaner with bleach. Rinse and let dry. Tip furniture on its side to drain, and towel-dry metal joints to prevent rust. Apply a thin coat of car wax to metal pieces to help repel stains. **Bounty with Dawn Paper Towels** are super-strong and have detergent built in. Just wet to activate it, then quickly wipe away stains and smudges on outdoor furniture to keep it ready to use all season long.

CUSHIONS

Check care labels to see if covers can be removed and machine-washed. Otherwise, spot-clean them with the dishwashing liquid–and–water solution used on furniture. Rinse with a cloth, and let dry.

Apply a weather-guarding spray, like **Scotchgard Heavy Duty Water Shield**, to keep fabric covers from fading and staining, and store them inside at night and when it rains.

PLANTS & GRASS

Before using any cleaners on your patio and deck, be sure to soak down nearby plants, bushes, and grass with water to keep detergent runoff from damaging them, or use a product like **Scotts® Outdoor Cleaner Plus OxiClean™**. It's formulated to clean and remove mildew from concrete, wood, and more without damaging lawns and plants.

WOOD DECKING

Take care of mold, mildew, and discoloration with a commercial deck cleaner. Test a small spot; then apply, wait, and hose off. Try Good Housekeeping Lab pick **30 Seconds® Outdoor Cleaner®**. Easy!

PATIO SURFACES

Erase leaf stains from concrete, brick, or stone with a specially formulated rust remover, like **Whink® Rust Oxy® Stain Remover.**

 1-MINUTE TIP! Close table umbrellas when not in use so they stay clean of dirt and debris.

KEEP YOUR GRILL SIZZLING

A clean BBQ not only looks nicer, but lasts longer and
cooks better-tasting food, too!

SPEED-CLEAN THE GRATES

Fire up the grill for a few minutes. Shut
it off, and, before it's completely cooled,
go over the grates with a heavy-duty
scrubbing pad to remove any food bits.
You can also do this right before you
start to cook, as the grill is heating. To
quickly clean already-cool grates, try
Good Housekeeping Lab pick **Parker &
Bailey BBQ Grill Cleaner & Degreaser**.
It works in just 2 minutes.

COVER GROUND

Place a barbecue pad under the grill to
keep grease stains off your patio. Mats
made of lightweight concrete and fiber,
like **DiversiTech® Original Grill Pad**,
breathe, so mildew isn't an issue as it is
with rubber and plastic types. Clean it
with a garden hose.

DITCH THE WIRE BRUSH

Don't use one of these to clean your grill. The bristles can break off, remain on the grates, and get into the food. Instead, use a stainless-steel mesh pad or, on a cool grill, a nylon brush, like **Char-Broil® Cool Cleaning Nylon Grill Brush**. Even a crumpled ball of aluminum foil works well.

GET A GRILL COVER

You'll never need to clean dirt, pollen, or bird droppings off your grill again. Plus, it protects your BBQ from the elements, which extends its life. Hose the cover clean as needed.

PREVENT STAINS

Protect wooden side tables from dribbles and drips with small, plastic cutting boards. They're also good for carrying utensils inside and right to the dishwasher. Keep a canister of cleaning wipes handy to nab splatters before they bake on and a spray bottle of water to douse flare-ups before they blacken the inside of the grill's hood.

TIPS FOR WINDOWS, GUTTERS & MORE

Whether you do them yourself or call in a pro, address these important tasks once (maybe twice) per year, and be done with them.

CLEAR OUT DEBRIS

Leaf-clogged gutters won't drain rainwater from your roof or handle snow as they are designed to. Most lawn services will do this job with a leaf blower if it's not something you can or want to do.

Good Housekeeping Seal Spotlight: Englert® LeafGuard® Rain Gutters are designed in one piece with a built-in cover that allows water to drain but deflects leaves and debris, which helps prevent clogs and reduces the need for cleaning.

WIPE BOTH WAYS

Dry windows vertically on one side and horizontally on the other. Then, when you see a streak, you'll know which side of the glass it's on.

REFRESH THE FIREPLACE

With a utility vacuum, suck up cold (at least four days old) ashes from the firebox. Dispose of them in a metal container away from the house. Brush, vacuum, or wet-clean the hearth and surrounding areas as needed. Call in a professional chimney sweep yearly to clean and inspect the chimney.

5 WINDOW CLEANING MISTAKES TO AVOID

Steer clear of these common errors so the sun shines in.

1 CHOOSING A SUNNY DAY. Do this job in the blazing sun and the cleaner will dry on the hot windows before you get to wipe it off, leaving a streaky mess. Instead, choose a dry, cloudy day. But if the sun's out and you're itching to clean, start with the windows on the coolest side of the house.

2 NOT DUSTING THE SILLS AND SASHES FIRST. Skip this step, and any liquid that drips onto the window frames will create a muddy mess. Always vacuum the frame, sill, and sash before tackling the glass.

3 NOT USING ENOUGH CLEANER. Don't be afraid to generously spritz your windows with cleaner, especially if they are extra dirty. You need plenty of cleaner to dissolve and suspend the dirt so it can be completely wiped away. Skimp, and you'll be seeing streaks. **Invisible Glass® Aerosol Glass Cleaner** has a no-drip formula, so it stays where you spray it for neat and easy cleaning.

4 USING NEWSPAPER TO DRY. Some folks swear by this trick, but it can be messy and ineffective. Instead, use microfiber cloths. They are super absorbent, washable, and leave the glass shiny and streak-free.

5 CHOOSING THE WRONG PAPER TOWEL. If a paper towel is still your cloth of choice, choose one that's up to the task. There's nothing worse than drying with a towel that separates or leaves lots of lint on the glass. In Good Housekeeping lab tests, **Bounty Regular Paper Towels** were strong when tested wet and dry, held up best, and didn't deposit lint on glass.

GOOD HOUSEKEEPING

CLEAN OUT YOUR CAR IN 15 MINUTES

These speedy cleaning tricks will have you riding in style in no time.

SORT AND TOSS

Go through the front, back, and trunk of the car, looking under the seats and in door pockets and holders. Toss any trash into a bag, and remove any items that don't belong in the car.

WIPE SURFACES

Clean the dashboard, door panels, armrests, consoles, and steering wheel with **Armor All® Cleaning Wipes**, baby wipes, or a damp cloth.

SHAKE MATS

Remove and shake out floor mats. With a handheld vacuum, go over the seats and the carpeting on the floor and in the trunk. Pressed for time? Use a lint roller to nab the most obvious specks.

It might be handy to use kitchen dishwashing liquid, but it's too harsh on a car's finish. Instead, use a product formulated specifically for automobiles. **Simple Green® Wash & Wax** cuts through dirt, grime, and even bugs to clean and leave behind a streak-free shine in one step.

ORGANIZE THE TRUNK

You can buy trunk-organizing bins or use a laundry basket to stash reusable grocery bags or clothes headed for the dry cleaner. Tuck a vinyl shower-curtain liner in there to spread out and keep your trunk clean when hauling plants and garden supplies, coolers, and beach items.

HEAD OFF A TRASH PILEUP

Fill an empty tissue box with plastic supermarket bags and stash it under a seat so it's handy whenever trash needs to be collected.

FRESHEN THE AIR

Combat stinky pet and telltale takeout food smells with air-freshening **Febreze Car Vent Clips**. Simply attach one to your car's dashboard vent. It's adjustable for more or less fragrance.

STAIN, STAIN GO AWAY

The longer a stain sets, the tougher it is to
remove. Treat stains on washable garments
(even with just a dab of cold water) as
quickly as you can. For dry-clean items,
bring them in within a couple of days.

STAIN RESCUE

"If I don't do laundry today, I'm gonna have to buy new clothes tomorrow."

—*Anna Paquin, actress*

Removing stains isn't as difficult as it might seem. With the right tools, some science, and a little luck thrown in for good measure, even the most challenging stains can become history. Because stain removal is likely one of the most troublesome problems, this chapter will arm you with all the necessary advice and steps to help you remove more than 60 common food, pet, and household stains from washable fabrics and water-safe upholstery and carpets. Keep it handy, refer to it often, and never cry over spilled milk again.

6 ESSENTIAL SUPPLIES

If you stock these products along with your regular laundry staples, then there's no stain you can't tackle.

1 ABSORBENT. Baking soda, cornstarch, cornmeal, talcum powder, or fuller's earth (available in pharmacies) can be used to absorb greasy stains.

2 ACETONE. Use pure acetone or non-oily nail-polish remover on stains like nail polish. Do not use acetone on fabrics containing acetate or triacetate—it will melt these fibers!

3 AMMONIA. Purchase the household version of ammonia, which works well on dried blood, perspiration, citrus juice, felt-tip pen, urine, and other acid-based stains. Note, however, that ammonia can damage silk and wool fibers.

4 DEGREASER OR ADHESIVE REMOVER. This is a general term describing solvent-based liquids and sprays that are particularly useful for candle wax, sticky residue, and oily or greasy stains. With any solvent, repeated light applications are more effective than one heavy dose. Always wash out the solvent completely before laundering any item treated with it, and air-dry until you are sure the solvent is removed.

5 ENZYME PRESOAKS. These products break down protein stains, such as blood, grass, and baby formula. A laundry detergent that contains enzymes can also be used for presoaking.

6 RUST REMOVER. Choose a commercial rust remover, available in supermarkets and hardware stores, for rust and yellow stains. Handle it carefully, and always follow package directions.

GH ON CALL

If you own an Amazon Alexa–enabled device, check out our free Good Housekeeping Stain Removal skill. It will walk you through step-by-step directions for removing food stains, pet stains, and more from washable fabrics, upholstery, and carpeting. Enjoy!

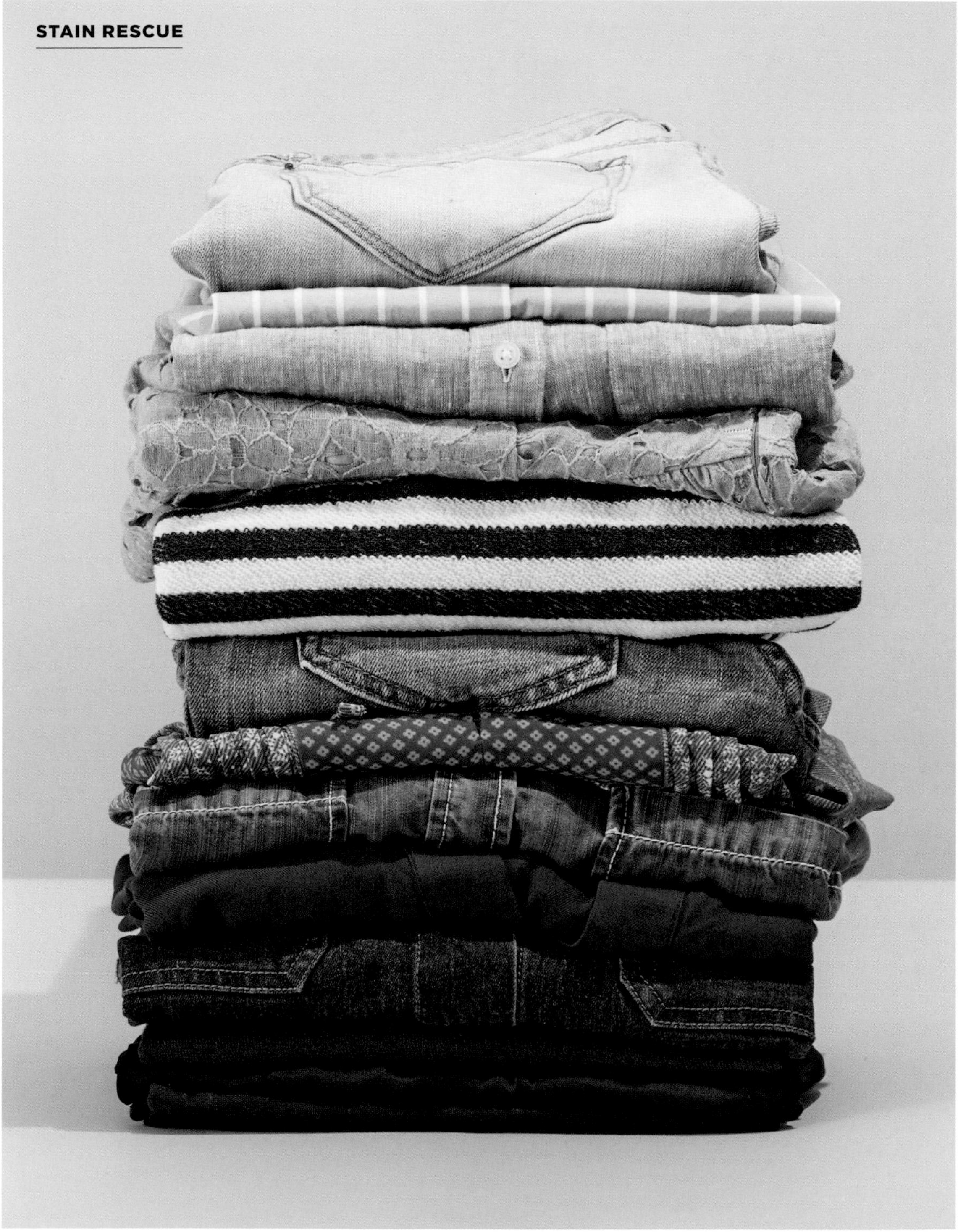

MASTER YOUR TECHNIQUE

How you work on stains is just as important as what
you use to remove them and assures that your fabric won't
be damaged in the process.

BLOT

Using a clean cloth, blotting lifts out stains and keeps them from penetrating deeper into the fabric. To keep the stain from spreading, begin blotting at the stain's outer edge and work toward the center. Blotting is especially important when working on carpet or upholstery, where you can't place an absorbent pad underneath the stain.

SPONGE

Place the stained item right-side up over an absorbent pad. Using a clean white cloth dampened with the stain-removal product, gently dab the area so the stain migrates out of the fabric and into the pad. To prevent restaining the area, change the absorbent pad frequently. Sponging with water may also be used as a final step to "rinse" other stain-removal products from upholstery and carpeting.

SCRAPE

For gloppy stains (think baby food, eggs, chocolate, ketchup), the goal is to get rid of the excess before attacking the stain itself. Use a dull knife or a spoon to gently remove the excess without harming the fabric, carpet, or upholstery.

TAMP

Tamping is an up-and-down motion using a bristled brush or the back of a spoon. The goal is to break up the hard shell of a stain, allowing the stain remover to penetrate.

 1-MINUTE TIP! Assemble a stain removal first-aid kit ahead of time so you're ready when spills happen. Include white cloths (cloth diapers work well) or paper towels for blotting, a spoon for scraping, carpet and upholstery cleaner, and a spray bottle of cold water for rinsing.

PRESOAK

This is an effective way to loosen heavy soils prior to laundering. You can do it in a basin, in the sink, or even in the washing machine. Mix the soaking agent with water and then add the item(s) to be soaked. Minimum soaking time is 30 minutes; maximum is usually overnight.

FREEZE

This is usually the first step in removing soft, pliable, or gooey substances, like chewing gum, rubber cement, and candle wax. Apply an ice cube wrapped in a small plastic bag to the stain. If the stained item is small enough, you can even pop it in the freezer for a few minutes. The goal is to harden the substance so most of it can be scraped off before additional treatment.

FLUSH

Put a clean absorbent pad or a layer of folded paper towels underneath the spot. Using an eyedropper, squeeze bottle, or spray bottle, apply the flushing agent slowly so it is absorbed into the pad, taking some of the stain with it. Change the pad as soon as you see traces of the stain. Flushing can also be done by holding the stained fabric under a faucet and letting water rush through it, or by placing the stained item facedown and on a pad and flushing from the back.

UPHOLSTERY CLEANING: KNOW THE CODES

The furniture industry has voluntary codes that indicate the appropriate cleaning methods for different types of upholstery fabrics. You'll usually find them printed on fabric samples, on a label under seat cushions, or on hang tags. Use these labels as a guide for safe spot removal and overall cleaning. If no code exists, try a cleaning method on a hidden spot or call a professional upholstery cleaner for advice.

WATER-BASED **W**

It is safe to use cleaning methods using water-based products, the foam from a mild detergent, or an upholstery shampoo. But use sparingly, and avoid over-wetting.

SOLVENT-BASED **S**

Water should not be used on fabrics labeled *S*. Check the list of contents on the label of any cleaner to ensure water is not in the product. Use solvent-based cleaners sparingly and in a well-ventilated room.

WATER OR SOLVENT-BASED **WS**

You're in luck: Either water or sovent-based cleaning methods are safe to use on this upholstery.

NEITHER WATER NOR SOLVENT-BASED **X**

If your label is marked with an *X*, it is time to call a professional. Clean this fabric yourself only by vacuuming or brushing it lightly to prevent accumulation of dust and grime.

CARPET CARE CAUTIONS

Protect your investment and make it easier to remove
stains with these supersmart strategies.

READ THE FINE PRINT.

Many carpets come with care information
and details about the types of stains and care
that the warranty does and does not cover.
Be sure to read it and put the information in a
safe place so you can find it when you need it.

ACT FAST.

Most of today's carpets are treated with
stain-resistant finishes, but that doesn't
mean they are stain-proof. These finishes
hold the spill on the fiber's surface, which
gives you time to clean it up before the stain
penetrates the tufts. The longer you leave the
spill unattended, the more difficult it
will be to remove.

BE PATIENT.

It's better and safer to remove stains
gradually using a small amount of cleaner
and lots of blotting. If it doesn't come out
the first time, try again. Never saturate
carpets with cleaner or water.

ZAP ODORS.

If you've got pets, you need to eliminate
the odors as well as the stains to keep them
from returning to the scene of the crime.
Choose a stain remover with enzymes that
kill odor-causing bacteria.

DEEP-CLEAN.

Every 12–18 months, have your carpet
professionally cleaned and the stain repellent
reapplied. Professional services do a more
thorough job than you can at home, and it's
often required by the carpeting manufacturer
in order to maintain the warranty.

STAINS A TO Z

These methods are for washable fabrics and water-safe upholstery and carpets. Test all solutions in a hidden spot for safety. For dry cleanables and other delicates, reach out to a professional.

ALCOHOLIC BEVERAGES

FABRIC

1 Sponge the stain with cool water or soak for about 30 minutes in a basin of cool water.

2 Pretreat with a prewash stain remover.

3 Launder. If it's safe for the fabric, add chlorine or oxygen bleach to the wash.

UPHOLSTERY

method 1

1 Mix 1 tablespoon white vinegar with ⅔ cup rubbing alcohol.

2 Using a clean white cloth, sponge the stain with the vinegar/alcohol solution.

3 Blot until the liquid is absorbed.

4 Repeat Steps 2 and 3 until the stain disappears.

method 2

1 Mix 1 tablespoon hand-dishwashing liquid with 2 cups cool water.

2 Using a clean white cloth, sponge the stain with the detergent solution.

3 Blot until the liquid is absorbed.

4 Repeat Steps 2 and 3 until the stain disappears.

5 Sponge with cold water to remove the detergent solution and blot dry.

CARPET

1 Blot up the spilled beverage.

2 Mix 1 tablespoon hand-dishwashing liquid and 1 tablespoon white vinegar with 2 cups warm water.

3 Using a clean white cloth, sponge the stain with the detergent/vinegar solution. Apply a little bit at a time, blotting frequently with a dry cloth until the stain disappears.

4 Sponge with cold water to remove the solution and blot dry.

APPLE JUICE OR APPLESAUCE

FABRIC

1 If applesauce, scrape off excess fruit.

2 Flush under cold running water.

3 Launder using the warmest water and type of bleach safe for the fabric.

UPHOLSTERY

1 If applesauce, scrape off excess fruit before blotting with a clean, dry cloth.

2 Mix 1 tablespoon hand-dishwashing liquid with 2 cups cool water.

3 Using a clean white cloth, sponge the stain with the detergent solution.

4 Blot until the liquid is absorbed.

5 Repeat Steps 3 and 4 until the stain disappears.

6 Sponge with cold water to remove the detergent solution and blot dry.

CARPET

1 If applesauce, scrape off excess fruit before blotting with a clean, dry cloth.

2 Mix 1 tablespoon hand-dishwashing liquid with 2 cups warm water.

3 Using a clean white cloth, sponge the stain with the solution.

4 Blot until the liquid is absorbed.

5 Repeat Steps 3 and 4 until the stain disappears or is no longer absorbed into the cloth.

6 If the stain remains, mix 1 tablespoon ammonia (caution, see page 150) with 2 cups warm water.

7 Sponge the stain with the ammonia solution. Blot until the liquid is absorbed.

8 Repeat Step 7 until the stain disappears.

9 Sponge with cold water and blot dry.

B

BARBECUE SAUCE

FABRIC

1 Working from the back of the stain, flush with cold water.

2 Pretreat with a liquid laundry detergent, then tamp the stain so the detergent penetrates, and let stand for several minutes.

3 Rinse well.

4 Sponge the stain with white vinegar and then rinse well.

5 Repeat Steps 2 through 4 until you have removed as much stain as possible.

6 Pretreat with a prewash stain remover and then launder with fabric-safe bleach.

7 If the stain remains, rub with a liquid laundry detergent and then soak in warm water for up to 30 minutes.

8 Launder with a fabric-safe bleach.

UPHOLSTERY

1 Mix 1 tablespoon hand-dishwashing liquid with 2 cups cool water.

2 Using a clean white cloth, sponge the stain with the detergent solution.

3 Blot until the liquid is absorbed.

4 Repeat Steps 2 and 3 until the stain disappears.

5 Sponge with cold water and blot dry.

CARPET

1 Mix 1 tablespoon hand-dishwashing liquid with 2 cups warm water.

2 Using a clean white cloth, sponge the stain with the detergent solution.

3 Blot until the liquid is absorbed.

4 Repeat Steps 2 and 3 until the stain disappears or is no longer absorbed into the cloth.

5 If the stain remains, mix 1 tablespoon ammonia (caution, see page 150) with ½ cup warm water.

6 Sponge the stain with the ammonia solution.

7 Blot until the liquid is absorbed.

8 Sponge with cold water and blot dry.

BERRIES

FABRIC

1 Flush the stain with cool water.

2 Mix 1 tablespoon white vinegar and ½ teaspoon liquid laundry detergent with 1 quart cool water.

3 Soak the stain in the vinegar/detergent solution for 15 minutes.

4 Rinse with cool water.

5 If the stain remains, sponge with rubbing alcohol and rinse thoroughly.

6 Launder using chlorine or oxygen bleach, if safe for the fabric.

UPHOLSTERY

1 Mix 1 tablespoon white vinegar with ⅔ cup rubbing alcohol.

2 Sponge the stain with a clean white cloth and the vinegar/alcohol solution.

3 Blot until the liquid is absorbed.

4 Repeat Steps 2 and 3 until the stain disappears.

5 Sponge with cold water and blot dry.

CARPET

1 Mix 1 tablespoon hand-dishwashing liquid with 2 cups warm water.

2 Using a clean white cloth, sponge the stain with the detergent solution.

3 Blot until the liquid is absorbed.

4 Repeat Steps 2 and 3 until the stain disappears or is no longer absorbed into the cloth.

5 If the stain remains, mix 1 tablespoon ammonia (caution, see page 150) with 2 cups cold water.

6 Sponge the stain with the ammonia solution.

7 Blot until the liquid is absorbed.

8 Sponge with cold water and blot dry.

BLOOD

FABRIC

1 If the stain is fresh, soak in cold water or use an eyedropper to apply hydrogen peroxide directly to the stain. For dried stains, brush the stain well to remove the surface deposit, then pretreat or soak in cool water with a laundry product containing enzymes.

2 Launder.

3 If the stain remains, rewash using fabric-safe bleach.

UPHOLSTERY

1 Mix 1 tablespoon hand-dishwashing liquid with 2 cups cold water. If the stain has dried, brush it well to remove any surface deposits.

2 Using a clean white cloth, sponge the stain with the detergent solution.

3 Blot until the liquid is absorbed.

4 Repeat Steps 2 and 3 until the stain disappears.

5 Sponge with cold water and blot dry.

CARPET

1 Mix 1 tablespoon hand-dishwashing liquid with 2 cups cold water. If the stain has dried, brush it well to remove any surface deposits.

2 Using a clean white cloth, sponge the stain with the detergent solution.

3 Blot until the liquid is absorbed.

4 Repeat Steps 2 and 3 until the stain disappears or is no longer absorbed into the cloth.

5 If the stain remains, mix 1 tablespoon ammonia (caution, see page 150) with ½ cup warm water.

6 Sponge the stain with the ammonia solution.

7 Blot until the liquid is absorbed.

8 Sponge with cold water and blot dry.

BUTTER

FABRIC

1 Scrape off excess butter.

2 Pretreat with a prewash stain remover.

3 Launder, using the hottest water safe for the fabric.

UPHOLSTERY

1 Scrape off excess butter.

2 Sprinkle baking soda, cornstarch, or other absorbent on the stain. Let stand for 10 to 15 minutes and then vacuum.

3 Using a clean white cloth, sponge the stain with a degreaser/adhesive remover.

4 Blot until the solvent is absorbed.

5 Repeat Steps 3 and 4 until the stain disappears.

6 Sponge with a mix of 1 tablespoon hand-dishwashing liquid and 2 cups cool water.

7 Sponge with cold water and blot dry.

CARPET

1 Scrape off excess butter.

2 Sprinkle baking soda, cornstarch, or other absorbent on the stain. Let stand for 10 to 15 minutes and then vacuum.

3 Using a clean white cloth, sponge the stain with a degreaser/adhesive remover.

4 Blot until the solvent is absorbed.

5 Repeat Steps 3 and 4 until the stain disappears or is no longer absorbed into the cloth.

6 If the stain remains, mix 1 tablespoon hand-dishwashing liquid and 1 tablespoon white vinegar with 2 cups warm water.

7 Sponge the stain with the detergent/vinegar solution.

8 Blot until the liquid is absorbed.

9 Sponge with cold water and blot dry.

C

CHEWING GUM

FABRIC

1 If the gum is still soft, freeze the item to harden the gum and then gently scrape off the excess.

2 Sponge with a degreaser/adhesive remover.

3 Pretreat with a prewash stain remover.

4 Launder.

UPHOLSTERY

1 If the gum is still soft, freeze it by directly applying an ice cube wrapped in a small plastic bag, then gently scrape off the excess.

2 Using a clean white cloth, sponge the stain with a degreaser/adhesive remover.

3 Blot until the solvent is absorbed.

4 Repeat Steps 2 and 3 until the stain disappears.

5 Sponge with a mix of 1 tablespoon hand-dishwashing liquid with 2 cups cool water.

6 Sponge with cold water and blot dry.

CARPET

1 If the gum is still soft, freeze it by directly applying an ice cube wrapped in a small plastic bag; gently scrape off excess gum.

2 Using a clean white cloth, sponge the stain with a degreaser/adhesive remover.

3 Blot until the solvent is absorbed.

4 Repeat Steps 2 and 3 until the stain disappears.

5 Sponge with a mix of 1 tablespoon hand-dishwashing liquid and 1 tablespoon of white vinegar with 2 cups warm water.

6 Blot until the liquid is absorbed.

7 Sponge with cold water and blot dry.

CANDLE WAX

FABRIC

1 If the wax is still soft, freeze the item to harden the wax and then scrape off the excess.

2 Sponge with a degreaser/adhesive remover.

3 Place the stain between clean paper towels and press with a warm iron to transfer the wax to the paper towels. Replace the paper towels frequently to absorb more wax and prevent the stain from transferring to other places on the fabric.

4 Pretreat with a prewash stain remover.

5 Launder with a fabric-safe bleach.

UPHOLSTERY

1 If the wax is still soft, freeze it by applying an ice cube wrapped in a small plastic bag and then gently scrape off the hardened excess.

2 Using a clean white cloth, sponge the stain with a degreaser/adhesive remover.

3 Blot until the solvent is absorbed.

4 Repeat Steps 2 and 3 until the stain disappears.

5 Sponge with a mix of 1 tablespoon hand-dishwashing liquid with 2 cups cool water.

6 Sponge with cold water and blot dry.

CARPET

1 If the wax is still soft, freeze it by applying an ice cube wrapped in a small plastic bag and then gently scrape off the hardened excess.

2 Sponge with a degreaser/adhesive remover.

3 Cover the stain with a clean white cloth and press with a warm iron, transferring the wax to the cloth. Repeat, using a clean portion of the cloth, until all the wax is transferred.

4 Sponge with a mix of 1 tablespoon hand-dishwashing liquid with 2 cups cool water.

5 Rinse with a cloth dipped in clear water; blot.

CHOCOLATE

FABRIC

1 Scrape off excess chocolate.

2 Pretreat with a prewash stain remover.

3 Launder.

4 If the stain remains, launder again using fabric-safe bleach.

UPHOLSTERY

method 1

1 Scrape off excess chocolate.

2 Mix 1 tablespoon hand-dishwashing liquid with 2 cups cool water.

3 Using a clean white cloth, sponge the stain with the detergent solution.

4 Blot until the liquid is absorbed.

5 Repeat Steps 3 and 4 until the stain disappears.

6 Sponge with cold water and blot dry.

method 2

1 Using a clean white cloth, sponge the stain with a degreaser/adhesive remover.

2 Blot until the solvent is absorbed.

3 Repeat Steps 1 and 2 until the stain disappears.

4 Sponge with a mix of 1 tablespoon hand-dishwashing liquid with 2 cups cool water.

5 Sponge with cold water and blot dry.

CARPET

1 Scrape off excess chocolate.

2 Mix 1 tablespoon hand-dishwashing liquid with 2 cups warm water.

3 Using a clean white cloth, sponge the stain with the detergent solution.

4 Blot until the liquid is absorbed.

5 Repeat Steps 3 and 4 until the stain disappears or is no longer absorbed into the cloth.

6 If the stain remains, mix 1 tablespoon ammonia (caution, see page 150) with 2 cups warm water.

7 Sponge the stain with the ammonia solution.

8 Blot until the liquid is absorbed.

9 Sponge with cold water and blot dry.

COFFEE

FABRIC

1 Sponge the stain with cool water, or soak the item for about 30 minutes in cool water.

2 Pretreat with a prewash stain remover.

3 Launder. If it's safe for the fabric, add chlorine bleach to the wash.

UPHOLSTERY

1 Mix 1 tablespoon hand-dishwashing liquid with 2 cups cool water.

2 Using a clean white cloth, sponge the stain with the detergent solution.

3 Blot until the liquid is absorbed.

4 Repeat Steps 2 and 3 until the stain disappears.

5 Sponge with cold water and blot dry.

CARPET

1 Blot up as much of the spilled coffee as possible.

2 Use plain water, or mix 1 tablespoon hand-dishwashing liquid and 1 tablespoon white vinegar with 2 cups warm water.

3 Using a clean white cloth, sponge the stain with the water or detergent/vinegar solution. Apply a little bit at a time, blotting frequently with a dry cloth until the stain disappears.

4 If using detergent/vinegar solution, sponge with cold water to remove the solution and blot dry.

COOKING OIL

FABRIC

1 Blot up excess oil.

2 Pretreat with a prewash stain remover.

3 Launder using the hottest water safe for the fabric.

UPHOLSTERY

1 Blot up excess oil.

2 Using a clean white cloth, sponge the stain with a degreaser/adhesive remover.

3 Blot until the solvent is absorbed.

4 Repeat Steps 2 and 3 until the stain disappears.

5 Sponge with a mix of 1 tablespoon hand-dishwashing liquid with 2 cups cool water.

6 Sponge with cold water and blot dry.

CARPET

1 Blot up excess oil.

2 Sprinkle baking soda, cornstarch, or other absorbent on the stain. Let stand for 10 to 15 minutes and then vacuum.

3 Using a clean white cloth, sponge the stain with a degreaser/adhesive remover.

4 Blot until the solvent is absorbed.

5 Repeat Steps 3 and 4 until the stain disappears or is no longer absorbed into the cloth.

6 Mix 1 tablespoon hand-dishwashing liquid with 2 cups warm water. Sponge the stain with this solution. Blot until the liquid is absorbed.

7 Sponge with cold water and blot dry.

CRANBERRY SAUCE

See Berries, page 160

CRAYON

FABRIC

1 If the crayon is soft, freeze the fabric to harden it and then scrape off the excess.

2 Place the stain between clean paper towels and press with a warm iron to transfer the stain to the paper towels. Replace the paper towels frequently to absorb more crayon and prevent the stain from transferring to other places on the fabric.

3 Pretreat with a prewash stain remover.

4 Launder with bleach that's appropriate for the fabric. If any color remains, rewash with bleach.

UPHOLSTERY

1 If the crayon is soft, freeze it by applying an ice cube wrapped in a small plastic bag and then scrape off the excess.

2 Using a clean white cloth, sponge the stain with a degreaser/adhesive remover.

3 Blot until the solvent is absorbed.

4 Repeat Steps 2 and 3 until the stain disappears.

5 Sponge with a mix of 1 tablespoon hand-dishwashing liquid with 2 cups cool water.

6 Sponge with cold water and blot dry.

CARPET

1 If the crayon is soft, freeze it by applying an ice cube wrapped in a small plastic bag and then scrape off the excess.

2 Cover the stain with a clean white cloth and press, using the tip of a warm iron. Repeat, using a clean portion of the cloth until all the wax is transferred from the carpet to the cloth.

3 If a color stain remains, sponge the stain with a degreaser/adhesive remover.

4 Sponge with a mix of 1 tablespoon hand-dishwashing liquid with 2 cups cool water.

5 Sponge with cold water and blot dry.

D

DIRT

FABRIC

1 Let dry if wet.

2 Brush off as much as possible.

3 Pretreat with a prewash stain remover.

4 Launder.

UPHOLSTERY

1 Let dry if wet.

2 Vacuum up as much as possible.

3 Mix 1 tablespoon hand-dishwashing liquid with 2 cups cool water.

4 Using a clean white cloth, sponge the stain with the detergent solution.

5 Blot until the liquid is absorbed.

6 Repeat Steps 4 and 5 until the stain disappears.

7 Sponge with cold water and blot dry.

CARPET

1 Let dry, if wet.

2 Vacuum up as much as possible.

3 Mix 1 tablespoon hand-dishwashing liquid with 2 cups warm water.

4 Using a clean white cloth, sponge the stain with the detergent solution.

5 Blot until the liquid is absorbed.

6 Repeat Steps 4 and 5 until the stain disappears.

7 Sponge with cold water and blot dry.

E

EGG

FABRIC

1 Scrape off excess egg.

2 Treat the stain with a prewash stain remover containing enzymes, or soak for at least 30 minutes using an enzyme laundry detergent.

3 Launder.

4 If the stain remains, let the item air-dry and then treat again with a prewash stain remover.

5 Launder, using chlorine or oxygen bleach, if safe for the fabric.

UPHOLSTERY

1 Scrape off excess egg.

2 Mix 1 tablespoon hand-dishwashing liquid with 2 cups cool water.

3 Using a clean white cloth, sponge the stain with the detergent solution.

4 Blot until the liquid is absorbed.

5 Repeat Steps 3 and 4 until the stain disappears.

6 Sponge with cold water and blot dry.

CARPET

1 Scrape off excess egg.

2 Mix 1 tablespoon hand-dishwashing liquid with 2 cups warm water.

3 Using a clean white cloth, sponge the stain with the detergent solution.

4 Blot until the liquid is absorbed.

5 Repeat Steps 3 and 4 until the stain disappears or is no longer absorbed into the cloth.

6 If the stain remains, mix 1 tablespoon ammonia (caution, see page 150) with 2 cups warm water.

7 Sponge the stain with the ammonia solution.

8 Blot until the liquid is absorbed.

9 Sponge with cold water and blot dry.

F

FECES

FABRIC

1 Pretreat or soak in warm water with a laundry product containing enzymes.

2 Launder, using chlorine or oxygen bleach, if safe for the fabric.

UPHOLSTERY

1 Mix 1 tablespoon hand-dishwashing liquid with 2 cups cool water.

2 Using a clean white cloth, sponge the stain with the detergent solution.

3 Blot until the liquid is absorbed.

4 Repeat Steps 2 and 3 until the stain disappears or is no longer absorbed into the cloth.

5 If the stain remains, use an eyedropper to apply hydrogen peroxide, then a drop or two of ammonia (caution, see page 150).

6 Sponge with cold water and blot dry.

CARPET

1 Mix 1 tablespoon hand-dishwashing liquid and 1 tablespoon white vinegar with 2 cups warm water.

2 Using a clean white cloth, sponge the stain with the detergent/vinegar solution.

3 Blot until the liquid is absorbed.

4 Repeat Steps 2 and 3 until the stain disappears or is no longer absorbed into the cloth.

5 If the stain remains, use an eyedropper to apply hydrogen peroxide, then a drop or two of ammonia (caution, see page 150).

6 Sponge with cold water and blot dry.

FELT-TIP MARKER

FABRIC

1 Place the stain facedown on clean paper towels.

2 Sponge rubbing alcohol into the area around the stain, and then apply it directly to the stain.

3 Continue sponging the stain with the alcohol, frequently changing the paper towels underneath, transferring as much ink as possible to the paper towels.

4 Or soak in mix of 1 gallon warm water, $1/4$ cup liquid laundry detergent, and $1/2$ cup ammonia for several hours or overnight. Scrub the stain several times.

5 Rinse thoroughly.

6 Launder with fabric-safe bleach.

UPHOLSTERY

1 Mix 1 tablespoon hand-dishwashing liquid and 1 tablespoon white vinegar with 2 cups cool water.

2 Using a clean white cloth, sponge the stain with the detergent/vinegar solution. Leave it on the stain for at least 30 minutes, blotting every 5 minutes with a clean white cloth and more solution.

3 Flush with cool water.

4 Blot until the liquid is absorbed.

5 Sponge the stain with rubbing alcohol. Blot to remove the stain.

6 Sponge with cold water.

7 Blot until the liquid is absorbed.

8 If the stain remains, mix 1 teaspoon hand-dishwashing liquid and 1 tablespoon ammonia (caution, see page 150) with 2 cups cool water. Sponge the stain with this solution. Leave it on the stain for at least 30 minutes, blotting every 5 minutes with a clean white cloth and more solution.

9 Sponge with cold water and blot dry.

CARPET

1 Mix 1 tablespoon hand-dishwashing liquid and 1 tablespoon white vinegar with 2 cups warm water.

2 Using a clean white cloth, sponge the stain with the detergent/vinegar solution, blotting frequently with a dry cloth until the stain disappears.

3 Sponge with clear water.

4 Blot until the liquid is absorbed.

5 If the stain remains, sponge the stain with rubbing alcohol. Blot to remove the stain.

6 Sponge with cold water.

7 Blot until the liquid is absorbed.

8 Mix 1 teaspoon hand-dishwashing liquid and 1 tablespoon ammonia (caution, see page 150) with 2 cups warm water. Sponge the stain with this solution. Leave it on the stain for at least 30 minutes, blotting every 5 minutes with a clean white cloth and more solution.

9 Sponge with cold water and blot dry.

FOUNDATION

See Makeup (Liquid), page 176

FRUIT PUNCH

FABRIC

1 Rinse thoroughly with cool water.

2 Pretreat with a heavy-duty laundry detergent.

3 Launder with fabric-safe bleach.

UPHOLSTERY

1 Mix 1 tablespoon hand-dishwashing liquid and 1 tablespoon white vinegar with 2 cups cool water.

2 Using a clean white cloth, sponge the stain with the detergent/vinegar solution. Leave it on the stain for at least 30 minutes, blotting every 5 minutes with a clean white cloth and more solution.

3 Sponge with cool water.

4 Blot until the liquid is absorbed.

5 Sponge the stain with rubbing alcohol. Blot to remove the stain.

6 Sponge with cold water.

7 If the stain remains, mix 1 teaspoon liquid hand-dishwashing detergent and 1 tablespoon ammonia (caution, see page 150) with 2 cups cool water. Sponge the stain with this solution. Leave it on the stain for at least 30 minutes, blotting every 5 minutes with a clean white cloth and more solution.

8 Sponge with cold water and blot dry.

CARPET

1 Mix 1 tablespoon hand-dishwashing liquid and 1 tablespoon white vinegar with 2 cups warm water.

2 Using a clean white cloth, sponge the stain with the detergent/vinegar solution. Leave it on the stain for at least 30 minutes, blotting every 5 minutes with a clean white cloth and more solution.

3 Sponge with warm water.

4 Blot until the liquid is absorbed.

5 Sponge the stain with rubbing alcohol. Blot to remove the stain.

6 Sponge with cold water.

7 If the stain remains, mix 1 teaspoon hand-dishwashing liquid and 1 tablespoon ammonia (caution, see page 150) with 2 cups warm water. Sponge the stain with this solution. Leave it on the stain for at least 30 minutes, blotting every 5 minutes with a clean white cloth and more solution.

8 Sponge with cold water and blot dry,

G

GRAPE JUICE

FABRIC

1 Flush the stain with cool water.

2 Mix 1 tablespoon white vinegar and 1/2 teaspoon liquid laundry detergent with 1 quart warm water. Soak in this solution for 15 minutes.

3 Rinse with water.

4 If the stain remains, sponge with rubbing alcohol and rinse thoroughly.

5 Launder with fabric-safe bleach.

UPHOLSTERY

1 Mix 1 tablespoon white vinegar with 2/3 cup rubbing alcohol.

2 Using a clean white cloth, sponge the stain with the vinegar/alcohol solution.

3 Blot until the liquid is absorbed.

4 Repeat Steps 2 and 3 until the stain disappears.

5 Sponge with cold water and blot dry.

CARPET

1 Mix 1 tablespoon liquid hand-dishwashing detergent with 2 cups warm water.

2 Using a clean white cloth, sponge the stain with the detergent solution.

3 Blot until the liquid is absorbed.

4 Repeat Steps 2 and 3 until the stain disappears or is no longer absorbed into the cloth

5 If the stain remains, mix 1 tablespoon ammonia (caution, see page 150) with 2 cups warm water.

6 Sponge the stain with the ammonia solution.

7 Blot until the liquid is absorbed.

8 Sponge with cold water and blot dry.

GRAVY

FABRIC

1 Scrape off excess.

2 Pretreat with a prewash stain remover.

3 Launder using the hottest water safe for the fabric.

UPHOLSTERY

1 Scrape off excess.

2 Sprinkle baking soda, cornstarch, or other absorbent on the stain. Let stand for 10 to 15 minutes, then vacuum.

3 Using with a clean white cloth, sponge the stain with degreaser/adhesive remover.

4 Blot until the solvent is absorbed.

5 Repeat Steps 3 and 4 until the stain disappears.

CARPET

1 Scrape off excess.

2 Sprinkle baking soda, cornstarch, or other absorbent on the stain. Let stand for 10 to 15 minutes, then vacuum.

3 Using a clean white cloth, sponge the stain with a degreaser/adhesive remover.

GRASS

FABRIC

1 Pretreat with a prewash stain remover, or rub liquid laundry detergent with enzymes into the stain.

2 Launder with fabric-safe bleach, using the hottest water safe for the fabric.

UPHOLSTERY

1 Using a clean white cloth, sponge the stain with acetone (caution, see page 150), if safe for the fabric.

2 If the stain remains, mix 1 tablespoon hand-dishwashing liquid with 2 cups cool water.

3 Sponge the stain with the detergent solution.

4 Blot until the liquid is absorbed.

5 Mix 1 tablespoon ammonia (caution, see page 150) with 2 cups cool water.

6 Sponge the stain with the ammonia solution.

7 Blot until the liquid is absorbed.

8 Sponge with cold water and blot dry.

CARPET

1 Using a clean white cloth, sponge the stain with acetone (caution, see page 150).

2 If the stain remains, mix 1 tablespoon hand-dishwashing liquid with 2 cups warm water.

3 Sponge the stain with the detergent solution.

4 Blot until the liquid is absorbed.

5 Mix 1 tablespoon ammonia (caution, see page 150) with 2 cups warm water.

6 Sponge the stain with the ammonia solution.

7 Blot until the liquid is absorbed.

8 Sponge with cold water and blot dry.

GRAVY continued

4 Blot until the solvent is absorbed.

5 Repeat Steps 3 and 4 until the stain disappears or is no longer absorbed into the cloth.

6 If the stain remains, mix 1 tablespoon hand-dishwashing liquid and 1 tablespoon white vinegar with 2 cups warm water. Sponge the stain with this solution. Blot until the liquid is absorbed.

7 Sponge with cold water to remove the detergent/vinegar solution and blot dry.

GREASE

FABRIC

1 Pretreat with a prewash stain remover or degreaser/adhesive remover.

2 Launder using the hottest water safe for the fabric.

UPHOLSTERY

1 Scrape off excess.

2 Sprinkle baking soda, cornstarch, or other absorbent on the stain. Let stand for 10 to 15 minutes, then vacuum.

3 Using a clean white cloth, sponge the stain with a degreaser/adhesive remover.

4 Blot until the solvent is absorbed.

5 Repeat Steps 3 and 4 until the stain disappears.

6 Sponge with a mix of 1 tablespoon hand-dishwashing liquid and 2 cups cool water.

7 Rinse and blot dry.

CARPET

1 Scrape off excess.

2 Sprinkle baking soda, cornstarch, or other absorbent on the stain. Let stand 10 to 15 minutes, then vacuum.

3 Using a clean white cloth, sponge the stain with a degreaser/adhesive remover.

4 Blot until the solvent is absorbed.

5 Mix 1 tablespoon liquid hand-dishwashing detergent and 1 tablespoon white vinegar with 2 cups warm water. Sponge the stain with this solution. Blot until the liquid is absorbed.

6 Sponge with cold water to remove the detergent/vinegar solution and blot dry.

I

ICE CREAM

FABRIC

1 Pretreat or soak using an enzyme laundry product. Soak for at least 30 minutes or several hours for older stains.

2 Launder.

UPHOLSTERY

1 Mix 1 tablespoon hand-dishwashing liquid with 2 cups cool water.

2 Using a clean white cloth, sponge the stain with the detergent solution.

3 Blot until the liquid is absorbed.

4 Repeat Steps 2 and 3 until the stain disappears.

5 Sponge with cold water and blot dry.

CARPET

1 Mix 1 tablespoon hand-dishwashing liquid with 2 cups warm water.

2 Using a clean white cloth, sponge the stain with the detergent solution.

3 Blot until the liquid is absorbed.

4 Repeat Steps 2 and 3 until the stain disappears or is no longer absorbed into the cloth.

5 If the stain remains, mix 1 tablespoon ammonia (caution, see page 150) with 2 cups warm water.

6 Sponge the stain with the ammonia solution.

7 Blot until the liquid is absorbed.

8 Sponge with cold water and blot dry.

INK, BALLPOINT

FABRIC

1 Sponge with rubbing alcohol until the ink stops bleeding.

2 Rinse thoroughly.

3 If the stain remains, rub liquid laundry detergent into the stain.

4 Launder with fabric-safe bleach.

UPHOLSTERY

1 Using a clean white cloth, sponge the stain with rubbing alcohol.

2 Blot until the ink and alcohol are absorbed.

3 Repeat Steps 1 and 2 until the stain disappears.

4 Sponge with a mix of 1 tablespoon liquid hand-dishwashing detergent with 2 cups cool water.

5 Rinse and blot dry.

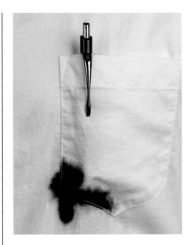

CARPET

1 Using a clean white cloth, sponge the stain with rubbing alcohol.

2 Blot until the ink and alcohol is absorbed.

3 Mix 1 tablespoon hand-dishwashing liquid and 1 tablespoon white vinegar with 2 cups warm water.

4 Sponge the stain with the detergent/vinegar solution.

5 Blot until the liquid is absorbed.

6 Repeat Steps 1 through 5 until the stain disappears.

7 Sponge with cold water and blot dry.

J

JELLY

FABRIC

1 Flush stain with cool water.

2 Mix 1 tablespoon white vinegar and 1/2 teaspoon liquid laundry detergent with 1 quart warm water. Soak in this solution for 15 minutes.

3 Rinse with water.

4 If the stain remains, sponge with rubbing alcohol and rinse thoroughly.

5 Launder, using fabric-safe bleach.

UPHOLSTERY

1 Mix 1 tablespoon white vinegar with 2/3 cup rubbing alcohol.

2 Using a clean white cloth, sponge the stain with the vinegar/alcohol solution.

3 Blot until the liquid is absorbed.

4 Repeat Steps 2 and 3 until the stain disappears.

5 Sponge with cold water and blot dry.

CARPET

1 Mix 1 tablespoon hand-dishwashing liquid with 2 cups warm water.

2 Using a clean white cloth, sponge the stain with the detergent solution.

3 Blot until the liquid is absorbed.

4 Repeat Steps 2 and 3 until the stain disappears or is no longer absorbed into the cloth.

5 If the stain remains, mix 1 tablespoon ammonia (caution, see page 150) with 2 cups warm water.

6 Sponge the stain with the ammonia solution.

7 Blot until the liquid is absorbed.

8 Sponge with cold water and blot dry.

K

KETCHUP

FABRIC

1 Working from the back of the stain, flush with cold water.

2 Pretreat with a liquid laundry detergent, then tamp the stain. Let stand for several minutes.

3 Rinse well.

4 Sponge with white vinegar.

5 Rinse well.

6 Repeat Steps 2 through 5 until you have removed as much of the stain as possible.

7 Pretreat with a prewash stain remover and then launder.

8 If the stain remains, rub with a liquid laundry detergent and then soak in warm water for up to 30 minutes.

9 Launder again, with fabric-safe bleach, if necessary.

UPHOLSTERY

1 Sponge with cool water.

2 Mix 1 tablespoon hand-dishwashing liquid with 2 cups cool water.

3 Using a clean white cloth, sponge the stain with the detergent solution.

4 Blot until the liquid is absorbed.

5 Repeat Steps 3 and 4 until the stain disappears.

6 Sponge with cold water and blot dry.

CARPET

1 Sponge with cool water.

2 Mix 1 tablespoon hand-dishwashing liquid with 2 cups warm water.

3 Using a clean white cloth, sponge the stain with the detergent solution.

4 Blot until the liquid is absorbed.

5 Repeat Steps 3 and 4 until the stain disappears or is no longer absorbed into the cloth.

6 If the stain remains, mix 1 tablespoon ammonia (caution, see page 150) with 1/2 cup warm water.

7 Sponge the stain with the ammonia solution.

8 Blot until the liquid is absorbed.

9 Sponge with cold water and blot dry.

L

LIPSTICK

FABRIC

1 Scrape off excess lipstick.

2 Pretreat with a prewash stain remover or a degreaser/adhesive remover.

3 Launder with fabric-safe bleach.

UPHOLSTERY

1 Scrape off excess lipstick.

2 Using a clean white cloth, sponge the stain with a degreaser/adhesive remover.

3 Blot until the solvent is absorbed.

4 Repeat Steps 2 and 3 until the stain disappears.

5 Sponge with a mix of 1 tablespoon liquid hand-dishwashing detergent with 2 cups cool water.

6 Sponge with cold water and blot dry.

CARPET

1 Scrape off excess lipstick.

2 Using a clean white cloth, sponge the stain with a degreaser/adhesive remover.

3 Blot until the solvent is absorbed.

4 Repeat Steps 2 and 3 until the stain disappears or is no longer absorbed into the cloth.

5 If the stain remains, mix 1 tablespoon hand-dishwashing liquid and 1 tablespoon white vinegar with 2 cups warm water.

6 Sponge the stain with the detergent/vinegar solution.

7 Blot until the liquid is absorbed.

8 Sponge with cold water and blot dry.

LIQUID MAKEUP

See Makeup (Liquid), below

LOTION (HAND, FACIAL, OR BODY)

FABRIC

1 Scrape off excess lotion.

2 Pretreat with a prewash stain remover.

3 Launder using the hottest water safe for the fabric.

UPHOLSTERY

1 Scrape off excess lotion.

2 Sprinkle baking soda, cornstarch, or other absorbent on the stain. Let stand for 10 to 15 minutes, then vacuum.

3 Using a clean white cloth, sponge the stain with a degreaser/adhesive remover.

4 Blot until the solvent is absorbed.

5 Repeat Steps 3 and 4 until the stain disappears.

6 Sponge with a mix of 1 tablespoon liquid hand-dishwashing detergent and 2 cups cool water.

7 Sponge with cold water and blot dry.

CARPET

1 Scrape off excess lotion.

2 Sprinkle baking soda, cornstarch, or other absorbent on the stain. Let stand for 10 to 15 minutes, then vacuum.

3 Using a clean white cloth, sponge the stain with a degreaser/adhesive remover.

4 Blot until the solvent is absorbed.

5 Repeat Steps 3 and 4 until the stain disappears or is no longer absorbed into the cloth.

6 Mix 1 tablespoon liquid hand-dishwashing detergent and 1 tablespoon white vinegar with 2 cups warm water. Sponge the stain with this solution. Blot until the liquid is absorbed.

7 Sponge with cold water and blot dry.

M

MAKEUP (LIQUID)

FABRIC

1 Sponge the stain with a degreaser/adhesive remover.

2 Pretreat with a prewash stain remover.

3 Launder with fabric-safe bleach.

UPHOLSTERY

1 Sponge the stain with a degreaser/adhesive remover.

2 Mix 1 tablespoon liquid hand-dishwashing detergent with 2 cups cool water.

3 Using a clean white cloth, sponge the stain with the detergent solution.

4 Blot until the liquid is absorbed.

5 Repeat Steps 1 through 3 until the stain disappears.

6 Sponge with cold water to rinse and blot dry.

CARPET

1 Sponge the stain with a degreaser/adhesive remover.

2 Mix 1 tablespoon hand-dishwashing liquid with 2 cups warm water.

3 Sponge the stain with the detergent solution.

4 Blot until the liquid is absorbed.

5 Mix 1 tablespoon ammonia (caution, see page 150) with ½ cup water.

6 Sponge the stain with the ammonia solution.

7 Blot until the liquid is absorbed.

8 If the stain remains, use a makeup-remover wipe or mix 1 teaspoon white vinegar with 1 cup warm water. Sponge the stain with this solution. Blot until the liquid is absorbed.

9 Sponge with cold water to rinse and blot dry.

MASCARA

FABRIC

1 Pretreat with a prewash stain remover.

2 Launder with fabric-safe bleach.

UPHOLSTERY

1 Mix 1 tablespoon liquid hand-dishwashing detergent with 2 cups cool water.

2 Using a clean white cloth, sponge the stain with the detergent solution.

3 Blot until the liquid is absorbed.

4 Repeat Steps 2 and 3 until the stain disappears.

5 Sponge with cold water and blot dry.

CARPET

1 Mix 1 tablespoon hand-dishwashing liquid with 2 cups warm water.

2 Sponge the stain with the detergent solution.

3 Blot until the liquid is absorbed.

4 Mix 1 tablespoon ammonia (caution, see page 150) with ½ cup water.

5 Sponge the stain with the ammonia solution.

6 Blot until the liquid is absorbed.

7 If the stain remains, use a makeup-remover wipe or mix 1 teaspoon white vinegar with

1 cup warm water. Sponge the stain with this solution. Blot until the liquid is absorbed.

8 Sponge with cold water and blot dry.

MILK

FABRIC

1 Pretreat or soak using an enzyme laundry product. Soak for at least 30 minutes; soak several hours for older stains.

2 Launder.

UPHOLSTERY

1 Mix 1 tablespoon hand-dishwashing liquid with 2 cups cool water.

2 Using a clean white cloth, sponge the stain with the detergent solution.

3 Blot until the liquid is absorbed.

4 Repeat Steps 2 and 3 until the stain disappears.

5 Sponge with cold water and blot dry.

CARPET

1 Mix 1 tablespoon hand-dishwashing liquid with 2 cups warm water.

2 Using a clean white cloth, sponge the stain with the detergent solution.

3 Blot until the liquid is absorbed.

MUSTARD

FABRIC

method 1

1 Scrape off excess mustard.

2 Rub glycerin into the stain with your fingertips and let sit for a few minutes.

3 Rinse with cool water.

4 Launder using the hottest water and type of bleach safe for the fabric.

method 2

1 Scrape off excess mustard.

2 Flush under cold running water to loo sen the stain.

3 Pretreat with a prewash stain remover.

4 Launder, using the hottest water and type of bleach safe for the fabric.

UPHOLSTERY

1 Scrape off excess mustard.

2 Mix 1 tablespoon liquid hand-dishwashing detergent with 2 cups cool water.

3 Using a clean white cloth, sponge the stain with the detergent solution.

4 Blot until the liquid is absorbed.

5 Repeat Steps 3 and 4 until the stain disappears.

6 Sponge with cold water to remove the detergent solution and blot dry.

CARPET

1 Scrape off excess mustard.

2 Mix 1 tablespoon hand-dishwashing liquid with 2 cups warm water.

3 Using a clean white cloth, sponge the stain with the detergent solution.

4 Blot until the liquid is absorbed.

5 Repeat Steps 3 and 4 until the stain disappears.

6 If the stain remains, mix 1 tablespoon ammonia (caution, see page 150) with 2 cups warm water.

7 Sponge the stain with the ammonia solution.

8 Blot until the liquid is absorbed.

9 Sponge with cold water to remove the ammonia solution and blot dry.

MILK continued

4 Repeat Steps 2 and 3 until the stain disappears or is no longer absorbed into the cloth.

5 If the stain remains, mix 1 tablespoon ammonia (caution, see page 150) with 2 cups warm water.

6 Sponge the stain with the ammonia solution.

7 Blot until the liquid is absorbed.

8 Sponge with cold water and blot dry.

MUD

FABRIC

1 Let the mud dry, then brush off as much as possible.

2 Pretreat with a prewash stain remover.

3 Launder.

UPHOLSTERY

1 Let the mud dry, then vacuum up as much as possible.

2 Mix 1 tablespoon hand-dishwashing liquid with 2 cups cool water.

3 Sponge the stain with a clean white cloth and the detergent solution.

4 Blot until the liquid is absorbed.

5 Repeat Steps 3 and 4 until the stain disappears.

6 Sponge with cold water and blot dry.

CARPET

1 Let the mud dry, then vacuum up as much as possible.

2 Mix 1 tablespoon hand-dishwashing liquid with 2 cups warm water.

3 Sponge the stain with a clean white cloth and the detergent solution.

4 Blot until the liquid is absorbed.

5 Repeat Steps 3 and 4 until the stain disappears.

6 Sponge with cold water and blot dry.

N

NAIL POLISH

FABRIC

1 Place the fabric facedown on a clean white cloth or paper towels, and blot with acetone (caution, see page 150).

2 Rinse with water.

3 Repeat Steps 1 and 2 until blotting no longer transfers the stain to the cloth or paper towels.

4 Apply a prewash stain remover.

5 Launder with fabric-safe bleach.

UPHOLSTERY

1 Carefully blot up excess polish.

2 Using an eyedropper, apply a small amount of acetone (caution, see page 150) to the stain.

3 Blot immediately.

4 Repeat Steps 2 and 3 until no more stain is removed.

5 If the stain remains, apply hydrogen peroxide. Use an eyedropper to apply the peroxide directly on the stain. Blot with a clean cloth.

6 Repeat step 5 until no more stain is removed.

7 Sponge with cold water to remove the hydrogen peroxide and blot dry.

CARPET

1 Carefully blot up excess polish.

2 Using an eyedropper, apply a small amount of acetone (caution, see page 150) to the stain.

3 Blot immediately.

4 Repeat Steps 2 and 3 until no more stain is removed.

5 If the stain remains, apply hydrogen peroxide. Use an eyedropper to apply the peroxide directly on the stain. Blot with a clean cloth.

6 Sponge with cold water and blot dry to remove the hydrogen peroxide.

ORANGE/JUICE

FABRIC

1 Scrape off or blot excess.

2 Flush under cold running water.

3 Launder, using the warmest water and type of bleach safe for the fabric.

UPHOLSTERY

1 Scrape off excess.

2 Mix 1 tablespoon hand-dishwashing liquid with 2 cups cool water.

3 Using a clean white cloth, sponge the stain with the detergent solution.

4 Blot until the liquid is absorbed.

5 Repeat Steps 3 and 4 until the stain disappears.

6 Sponge with cold water and blot dry.

CARPET

1 Scrape off or blot excess.

2 Mix 1 tablespoon hand-dishwashing liquid with 2 cups warm water.

3 Using a clean white cloth, sponge the stain with the detergent solution.

4 Blot until the liquid is absorbed.

5 Repeat Steps 3 and 4 until the stain disappears or is no longer absorbed into the cloth.

6 If the stain remains, mix 1 tablespoon ammonia (caution, see page 150) with 2 cups warm water.

7 Sponge the stain with the ammonia solution.

8 Blot until the liquid is absorbed.

9 Sponge with cold water and blot dry.

P

PAINT, LATEX (ACRYLIC/ WATER-BASED)

FABRIC

1 Scrape off excess.

2 Working from the back of the fabric, flush the stain under warm running water.

3 Mix a solution of 1 part hand-dishwashing liquid to 1 part warm water.

4 Sponge the stain with the detergent solution, tamping it vigorously.

5 Rinse.

6 Repeat Steps 4 and 5 until no more paint is removed.

7 If the stain remains, try blotting with acetone (caution, see page 150).

8 Launder with fabric-safe bleach.

UPHOLSTERY

1 Scrape off excess.

2 Mix a solution of 1 part hand-dishwashing liquid to 1 part cool water.

3 Sponge the stain with the detergent solution, tamping it vigorously.

4 Rinse.

5 Repeat Steps 3 and 4 until no more paint is removed.

6 If the stain remains, try blotting with acetone (caution, see page 150).

7 Sponge with a mix of 1 tablespoon hand-dishwashing liquid with 2 cups cool water.

8 Sponge with cold water and blot dry.

CARPET

1 Scrape off excess paint.

2 Starting at the outer edge of the stain, apply acrylic paint and varnish remover (available at hardware and paint stores). Gently scrape away the paint as it softens. Repeat, using the remover sparingly, until you have removed as much paint as possible.

3 Sponge the stain with a mild solution of hand-dishwashing liquid and water. Tamp vigorously to break up the stain and allow the detergent to penetrate.

4 Blot until the liquid is absorbed.

5 Sponge with a solution of 1 part white vinegar to ten parts water.

6 Blot until the liquid is absorbed.

7 Sponge with cold water and blot dry.

PAINT, OIL-BASED

FABRIC

For fresh stains

1 Scrape off excess.

2 Using a clean white cloth, blot up as much paint as possible.

3 Rinse. DO NOT let the fabric dry.

4 Place the stain facedown on a stack of white paper towels or cloths. Blot with turpentine or paint thinner. Tamp the stain. Repeat, replacing the paper towels or cloth until no more paint can be removed.

5 Treat the remaining stain with hand-dishwashing liquid and soak overnight.

6 Rinse well.

7 Treat with a prewash stain remover and launder with fabric-safe bleach.

For old stains

1 Soften the stain by treating it with turpentine or paint thinner.

2 Once the paint has softened, treat as for fresh stains (Steps 4 through 7 above).

UPHOLSTERY AND CARPET

For fresh stains

1 Scrape off excess.

2 Using a clean white cloth, blot up as much paint as possible.

3 Using a clean white cloth, blot the stain with turpentine. Tamp the stain.

4 Keep applying turpentine to the stain, tamping and blotting until the paint is removed.

5 Mix 1 tablespoon hand-dishwashing liquid with 2 cups cool water.

6 Using a clean white cloth, sponge the stain with the detergent solution.

7 Blot until the liquid is absorbed.

8 Repeat Steps 6 and 7 until the stain disappears.

9 Sponge with cold water to remove the detergent solution and blot dry.

For old stains

1 Soften the stain by treating it with turpentine or paint thinner.

2 Once the paint has softened, treat as for fresh stains, Steps 3 through 9 above.

PENCIL LEAD

FABRIC

1 Use a soft eraser to remove the excess.

2 Pretreat with a prewash stain remover.

3 Launder with fabric-safe bleach.

UPHOLSTERY

1 Use a soft eraser to remove the excess.

2 Mix 1 tablespoon hand-dishwashing liquid with 2 cups cool water.

3 Using a clean white cloth, sponge the stain with the detergent solution.

4 Blot until the liquid is absorbed.

5 Sponge the stain with ammonia (caution, see page 150). Blot until the liquid is absorbed.

6 Repeat Steps 3 through 5 until the stain disappears.

7 Sponge with cold water and blot dry.

CARPET

1 Use a soft eraser to remove the excess.

2 Mix 1 tablespoon hand-dishwashing liquid with 2 cups warm water.

3 Using a clean white cloth, sponge the stain with the detergent solution.

4 Blot until the liquid is absorbed.

5 Sponge the stain with ammonia (caution, see page 150). Blot until the liquid is absorbed.

6 Repeat Steps 3 through 5 until the stain disappears.

7 Sponge with cold water and blot dry.

PERFUME

FABRIC

1 Pretreat with a prewash stain remover.

2 Launder.

UPHOLSTERY

1 Blot up excess perfume.

2 Using a clean white cloth, sponge the stain with a degreaser/adhesive remover.

3 Blot until the solvent is absorbed.

4 Repeat Steps 2 and 3 until the stain disappears.

5 Sponge with a mix of 1 tablespoon hand-dishwashing liquid with 2 cups cool water.

6 Sponge with cold water and blot dry.

CARPET

1 Blot up excess perfume.

2 Mix 1 tablespoon hand-dishwashing liquid and 1 tablespoon white vinegar with 2 cups warm water.

3 Using a clean white cloth, sponge the stain with the detergent/vinegar solution.

4 Blot until the liquid is absorbed.

5 Sponge with cold water and blot dry.

PERSPIRATION

FABRIC

1 Check to see if the stain has changed the color of the fabric. If so, apply ammonia (caution, see page 150) to fresh stains; apply white vinegar to old ones. Rinse.

2 Pretreat with a prewash stain remover, or rub liquid enzyme detergent into the stain.

3 Launder using the hottest water safe for the fabric. Stubborn stains may also respond to chlorine or oxygen bleach in the hottest water safe for the fabric.

UPHOLSTERY

1 Mix 1 teaspoon liquid hand-dishwashing detergent and 1 tablespoon ammonia (caution, see page 150) with 2 cups cool water.

2 Using a clean white cloth, sponge the stain with the detergent/ammonia solution.

3 Blot until the liquid is absorbed.

4 Mix 1 tablespoon liquid hand-dishwashing detergent and 1 tablespoon white vinegar with 2 cups cool water.

5 Sponge the stain with the detergent/vinegar solution.

6 Sponge with cold water and blot dry.

CARPET

Although perspiration stains may appear on the back and arms of upholstered furniture, the chances of these stains occurring on your carpet are very slim. In the unlikely event that this happens, use the same method as for upholstery.

PET STAINS

See Urine, page 191

See Feces, page 169

PINE RESIN

FABRIC

1 Sponge the stained area with or soak it in degreaser/adhesive remover; let it air-dry.

2 Soak the stain in a solution of 1 cup liquid laundry detergent and a few drops of ammonia (caution, see page 150) for at least 30 minutes.

3 Launder in the hottest water safe for the fabric with fabric-safe bleach.

UPHOLSTERY

1 Using a clean white cloth, sponge the stain with a degreaser/adhesive remover.

2 Tamp the stain to break it up and allow the stain remover to penetrate.

3 Blot until the liquid is absorbed.

4 If the stain remains, sponge with turpentine.

5 Mix 1 tablespoon hand-dishwashing liquid with 2 cups cool water.

6 Sponge the stain with the detergent solution.

7 Blot until the liquid is absorbed.

8 Repeat, alternating applications of turpentine and detergent solution, until the stain disappears.

9 Sponge with cold water and blot dry.

CARPET

1 Using a clean white cloth, sponge the stain with a degreaser/adhesive remover.

2 Tamp the stain.

3 Blot until the liquid is absorbed.

4 If the stain remains, sponge with turpentine.

5 Mix 1 tablespoon hand-dishwashing liquid with 2 cups warm water.

6 Sponge the stain with the detergent solution.

7 Blot until the liquid is absorbed.

8 Repeat, alternating applications of turpentine and detergent solution, until the stain disappears.

9 Sponge with cold water and blot dry.

POLLEN

FABRIC

1 Gently shake the garment to remove as much pollen as you can.

2 Use the sticky side of a piece of tape to carefully lift off the remaining particles, or vacuum lightly to pull particles out of the fabric. Avoid rubbing particles in.

3 Pretreat with a prewash stain remover.

4 Launder with fabric-safe bleach.

UPHOLSTERY

1 Vacuum up the pollen particles.

2 Use the sticky side of a piece of tape to carefully lift off the remaining particles.

3 Using a clean white cloth, sponge the stain with a degreaser/adhesive remover.

4 Blot until the solvent is absorbed.

5 Repeat Steps 3 and 4 until the stain disappears.

6 Sponge with a mix of 1 tablespoon hand-dishwashing liquid and 2 cups cool water.

7 Sponge with cold water and blot dry.

CARPET

1 Vacuum up the pollen particles.

2 Use the sticky side of a piece of tape to carefully lift off the remaining particles.

3 Using a clean white cloth, sponge the stain with a degreaser/adhesive remover.

4 Blot until the solvent is absorbed.

5 Repeat Steps 3 and 4 until the stain disappears.

6 Sponge with a mix of 1 tablespoon hand-dishwashing liquid and 2 cups cool water.

7 Sponge with cold water and blot dry.

R

RASPBERRIES

See Berries, page 160

RUST

FABRIC

A commercial rust remover (available in supermarkets and hardware stores) is the best way to remove rust. Because these products contain strong acids, caution is required. Be sure to read and follow the label directions carefully.

UPHOLSTERY AND CARPET

For small spots, try a commercial rust remover. For large or stubborn spots, call in a professional cleaner.

S

SAP

See Pine Resin, page 184

SHOE POLISH

FABRIC

method 1

1 Pretreat with a prewash stain remover.

2 Apply liquid enzyme laundry detergent and tamp the stain.

3 Launder in the hottest water safe for the fabric.

method 2

1 Using a clean white cloth, sponge the stain with a degreaser/adhesive remover.

2 Blot until the solvent is absorbed.

3 Repeat Steps 1 and 2 until the stain disappears.

4 Pretreat or rub in liquid laundry detergent.

5 Launder in the hottest water safe for the fabric with fabric-safe bleach.

UPHOLSTERY

1 Scrape off as much polish as possible.

2 Using a clean white cloth, sponge the stain with a degreaser/adhesive remover.

3 Blot until the solvent is absorbed.

4 Repeat Steps 2 and 3 until the stain disappears.

SALAD DRESSING
(CREAMY OR VINAIGRETTE)

FABRIC

1 Pretreat with a prewash stain remover.

2 Launder using the hottest water safe for the fabric.

UPHOLSTERY

1 Scrape off excess salad dressing.

2 Sprinkle baking soda, cornstarch, or other absorbent on the stain. Let stand for 10 to 15 minutes, then vacuum.

3 Using a clean white cloth, sponge the stain with a degreaser/adhesive remover.

4 Blot until the solvent is absorbed.

5 Repeat Steps 3 and 4 until the stain disappears.

6 Sponge with a mix of 1 tablespoon hand-dishwashing liquid with 2 cups cool water.

7 Sponge with cold water and blot dry.

CARPET

1 Scrape off excess salad dressing.

2 Sprinkle baking soda, cornstarch, or other absorbent on the stain. Let stand for 10 to 15 minutes, then vacuum.

3 Using a clean white cloth, sponge the stain with a degreaser/adhesive remover.

4 Blot until the solvent is absorbed.

5 If the stain remains, mix 1 tablespoon hand-dishwashing liquid and 1 tablespoon white vinegar with 2 cups warm water.

6 Using a white cloth, sponge the stain with the detergent/vinegar solution.

7 Blot until the liquid is absorbed.

8 Sponge with cold water and blot dry.

SHOE POLISH continued

5 Sponge with a mix of 1 tablespoon liquid hand-dishwashing detergent and 2 cups cool water.

6 Sponge with cold water and blot dry.

CARPET

1 Scrape off as much polish as possible.

2 Sponge the stain with a degreaser/adhesive remover.

3 Blot until the liquid is absorbed.

4 Mix 1 tablespoon hand-dishwashing liquid and 1 tablespoon ammonia (caution, see page 150) with 2 cups warm water.

5 Using a clean white cloth, sponge the stain with the detergent/ammonia solution.

6 Blot until the liquid is absorbed.

7 Sponge with cold water and blot dry.

SOFT DRINKS

FABRIC

1 Sponge the spot with cool water, or soak for about 30 minutes in a basin of cool water.

2 Pretreat with a prewash stain remover.

3 Launder with fabric-safe bleach.

UPHOLSTERY

1 Blot up as much of the spilled drink as possible.

2 Mix 1 tablespoon hand-dishwashing liquid with 2 cups cool water.

3 Using a clean white cloth, sponge the stain with the detergent solution.

4 Blot until the liquid is absorbed.

5 Repeat Steps 3 and 4 until the stain disappears.

6 Sponge with cold water and blot dry.

CARPET

1 Blot up as much of the spilled drink as possible.

2 Use plain water or mix 1 tablespoon hand-dishwashing liquid and 1 tablespoon white vinegar with 2 cups warm water.

3 Using a clean white cloth, sponge the stain with plain water or the detergent/vinegar solution. Apply a little bit at a time, blotting frequently with a dry cloth until the stain disappears.

4 Sponge with cold water and blot dry.

SOY SAUCE

FABRIC

1 Flush the stain with cold running water.

2 Sponge with ammonia (caution, see page 150) and rinse until you have removed as much stain as possible.

3 Pretreat with a prewash stain remover.

4 Launder with fabric-safe bleach.

UPHOLSTERY

1 Mix 1 tablespoon hand-dishwashing liquid with 2 cups cool water.

2 Sponge the stain with a clean white cloth and the detergent solution.

3 Blot until the liquid is absorbed.

4 Repeat Steps 2 and 3 until the stain disappears.

5 Sponge with cold water and blot dry.

CARPET

1 Mix 1 tablespoon hand-dishwashing liquid with 2 cups warm water.

2 Sponge the stain with a clean white cloth and the detergent solution.

3 Blot until the liquid is absorbed.

4 If the stain remains, mix 1 tablespoon ammonia (caution, see page 150) with 1/2 cup water.

5 Sponge the stain with the ammonia solution.

6 Blot until the liquid is absorbed.

7 Sponge with cold water and blot dry.

SPAGHETTI SAUCE

FABRIC

1 Working from the back of the stain, flush with cool water.

2 Pretreat with a liquid laundry detergent; tamp the stain and let stand for several minutes.

3 Rinse well.

4 Sponge with white vinegar.

5 Rinse well.

6 Repeat steps 2 through 5 until you have removed as much stain as possible.

7 Pretreat with a prewash stain remover.

8 Launder with fabric-safe bleach.

UPHOLSTERY

1 Using a clean white cloth, apply a degreaser/adhesive remover to the stained area.

2 Blot until the liquid is absorbed.

3 Repeat, applying and blotting the solution until the stain disappears or is no longer absorbed onto the cloth.

4 If the stain remains, mix 1 tablespoon hand-dishwashing liquid with 2 cups cool water.

5 Using a clean white cloth, sponge the stain with the detergent solution.

6 Blot until the liquid is absorbed.

7 Repeat Steps 5 and 6 until the stain disappears.

8 Sponge with cold water and blot dry.

CARPET

1 Mix 1 tablespoon hand-dishwashing liquid with 2 cups cool water.

2 Using a clean white cloth, sponge the stain with the detergent solution.

3 Blot until the liquid is absorbed.

4 If the stain remains, mix 1 tablespoon ammonia (caution, see page 150) with 1/2 cup cool water.

5 Sponge the stain with the ammonia solution.

6 Blot until the liquid is absorbed.

7 Sponge with cold water to remove the ammonia solution and blot dry.

STRAWBERRIES

FABRIC

1 Flush the stain with cool water.

2 Mix 1 tablespoon white vinegar and 1/2 teaspoon liquid laundry detergent with 1 quart cool water. Soak in this solution for 15 minutes.

3 Rinse with water.

4 If the stain remains, sponge with rubbing alcohol and rinse thoroughly.

5 Launder with fabric-safe bleach.

UPHOLSTERY

1 Mix 1 tablespoon white vinegar with 2/3 cup rubbing alcohol.

2 Using a clean white cloth, sponge the stain with the vinegar/alcohol solution.

3 Blot until the liquid is absorbed.

4 Repeat Steps 2 and 3 until the stain disappears.

5 Sponge with a mix of 1 tablespoon liquid hand-dishwashing detergent with 2 cups cool water.

6 Sponge with cold water and blot dry.

CARPET

1 Mix 1 tablespoon hand-dishwashing liquid with 2 cups cool water.

2 Using a clean white cloth, sponge the stain with the detergent solution.

3 Blot until the liquid is absorbed.

4 Repeat Steps 2 and 3 until the stain disappears or is no longer absorbed into the cloth.

5 If the stain remains, mix 1 tablespoon ammonia (caution, see page 150) with 2 cups cold water.

6 Sponge the stain with the ammonia solution.

7 Blot until the liquid is absorbed.

8 Sponge with cold water and blot dry.

SUNTAN LOTION

FABRIC

1 Scrape off excess lotion.

2 Pretreat with a prewash stain remover.

3 Launder, using the hottest water safe for the fabric.

UPHOLSTERY

1 Scrape off excess lotion.

2 Sprinkle baking soda, cornstarch, or other absorbent on the stain. Let stand for 10 to 15 minutes, then vacuum.

3 Using a clean white cloth, sponge the stain with a degreaser/adhesive remover.

4 Blot until the solvent is absorbed.

5 Repeat Steps 3 and 4 until the stain disappears.

6 Sponge with a mix of 1 tablespoon hand-dishwashing liquid with 2 cups cool water.

7 Sponge with cold water and blot dry.

CARPET

1 Scrape off excess lotion.

2 Sprinkle baking soda, cornstarch, or other absorbent on the stain. Let stand for 10 to 15 minutes, then vacuum.

3 Using a clean white cloth, sponge the stain with a degreaser/adhesive remover.

4 Blot until the solvent is absorbed.

5 If the stain remains, mix 1 tablespoon hand-dishwashing liquid and 1 tablespoon white vinegar with 2 cups warm water.

6 Using a clean white cloth, sponge the stain with the detergent/vinegar solution.

7 Blot until the liquid is absorbed.

8 Sponge with cold water and blot dry.

T

TAPE (ADHESIVE RESIDUE)

FABRIC

1 Scrape off excess residue.

2 If some sticky residue remains, rub waterless hand cleaner into the stain and then gently roll off the bits of adhesive, or work in a degreaser/adhesive remover until the residue dissolves.

3 Pretreat with a prewash stain remover.

4 Launder in the hottest water safe for the fabric.

UPHOLSTERY

1 Scrape off excess residue.

2 Using a clean white cloth, sponge the stain with a degreaser/adhesive remover.

3 Blot until the solvent is absorbed.

4 Repeat Steps 2 and 3 until the stain disappears.

5 Sponge with a mix of 1 tablespoon hand-dishwashing liquid with 2 cups cool water.

6 Sponge with cold water and blot dry.

CARPET

1 Scrape off excess residue.

2 Using a clean white cloth, sponge the stain with a degreaser/adhesive remover.

3 Blot until the solvent is absorbed.

4 Mix 1 tablespoon hand-dishwashing liquid and 1 tablespoon white vinegar with 2 cups warm water.

5 Sponge the stain with the detergent/vinegar solution.

6 Blot until the liquid is absorbed.

7 Sponge with cold water and blot dry.

TEA

FABRIC

1 Sponge the spot with cool water, or soak for about 30 minutes in a basin of cool water.

2 Pretreat with prewash stain remover.

3 Launder with fabric-safe bleach.

UPHOLSTERY

1 Sponge the stain with cool water.

2 Mix 1 tablespoon hand-dishwashing liquid with 2 cups cool water.

3 Using a clean white cloth, sponge the stain with the detergent solution.

4 Blot until the liquid is absorbed.

5 Repeat Steps 2 and 3 until the stain disappears.

6 Sponge with cold water and blot dry.

CARPET

1 Blot up the spilled tea and sponge the stain with cool water.

2 Mix 1 tablespoon hand-dishwashing liquid and 1 tablespoon white vinegar with 2 cups warm water.

3 Using a clean white cloth, sponge with plain water or the detergent/vinegar solution. Apply a little bit at a time, blotting frequently with a dry cloth until the stain disappears.

4 Sponge with cold water and blot dry.

TOMATO JUICE/ PASTE/SAUCE

FABRIC

1 Working from the back of the stain, flush with cold water.

2 Pretreat with a liquid laundry detergent, tamp the stain, and let stand for several minutes.

3 Rinse well.

4 Sponge with white vinegar.

5 Rinse well.

6 Repeat Steps 2 through 5 until you have removed as much stain as possible.

7 Pretreat with prewash stain remover.

8 Launder with fabric-safe bleach.

UPHOLSTERY

1 Mix 1 tablespoon hand-dishwashing liquid with 2 cups cool water.

2 Using a clean white cloth, sponge the stain with the detergent solution.

3 Blot until the liquid is absorbed.

4 Repeat Steps 2 and 3 until the stain disappears.

5 Sponge with cold water and blot dry.

CARPET

1 Mix 1 tablespoon hand-dishwashing liquid with 2 cups cool water.

2 Using a clean white cloth, sponge the stain with the detergent solution.

3 Blot until the liquid is absorbed.

4 Repeat Steps 2 and 3 until the stain disappears or is no longer absorbed into the cloth.

5 If the stain remains, mix 1 tablespoon ammonia (caution, see page 150) with 1/2 cup cool water.

6 Sponge the stain with the ammonia solution.

7 Blot until the liquid is absorbed.

8 Sponge with cold water and blot dry.

U

URINE

FABRIC

1 Pretreat or soak in warm water with an enzyme laundry product or a liquid laundry detergent containing enzymes.

2 Launder with fabric-safe bleach.

UPHOLSTERY

1 Mix 1 tablespoon hand-dishwashing liquid and 2 cups cool water.

2 Using a clean white cloth, sponge the stain with the detergent solution.

3 Blot until the liquid is absorbed.

4 Repeat Steps 2 and 3 until the stain disappears.

5 If the stain remains, use an eye dropper to apply hydrogen peroxide, then add a drop or 2 of ammonia (caution, see page 150).

6 Sponge with cold water and blot dry.

CARPET

1 Mix 1 tablespoon hand-dishwashing liquid and 1 tablespoon white vinegar with 2 cups warm water.

2 Using a clean white cloth, sponge the stain with the detergent/vinegar solution.

3 Blot until the liquid is absorbed.

4 If the stain remains, use an eyedropper to apply hydrogen peroxide, then add a drop or 2 of ammonia (caution, see page 150).

5 Sponge with cold water and blot dry.

VOMIT

FABRIC

1 Scrape off excess.

2 Pretreat with a prewash stain remover.

3 Launder using the hottest water safe for the fabric.

UPHOLSTERY

1 Scrape off excess.

2 Using a clean white cloth, sponge the stain with a degreaser/adhesive remover.

3 Blot until the solvent is absorbed.

4 Repeat Steps 2 and 3 until the stain disappears.

5 Sponge with a mix of 1 tablespoon hand-dishwashing liquid and 2 cups cool water.

6 Sponge with cold water and blot dry.

CARPET

1 Scrape off excess.

2 Using a clean white cloth, sponge the stain with a degreaser/adhesive remover.

3 Blot until the solvent is absorbed.

4 If the stain remains, mix 1 tablespoon hand-dishwashing liquid and 1 tablespoon white vinegar with 2 cups warm water. Sponge the stain with this solution. Blot until the liquid is absorbed.

5 Sponge with cold water and blot dry to remove the detergent/vinegar solution.

W

WINE, RED

FABRIC

1 Sponge the spot with cool water, or soak for about 30 minutes in a basin of cool water.

2 Pretreat with prewash stain remover.

3 Launder with fabric-safe bleach.

UPHOLSTERY

1 Blot up the spilled wine.

2 Sponge the stain with cold water.

3 Mix 1 tablespoon hand-dishwashing liquid and 1 tablespoon white vinegar with 2 cups cool water.

4 With a clean cloth, sponge the stain with the detergent/vinegar solution.

5 Blot until the liquid is absorbed.

6 Repeat Steps 3 and 4 until the stain disappears.

7 Sponge with cold water and blot dry.

CARPET

1 Blot up the spilled wine.

2 Sponge the stain with cold water.

3 Mix 1 tablespoon hand-dishwashing liquid and 1 tablespoon white vinegar with 2 cups warm water.

4 Using a clean white cloth, sponge the stain the detergent/vinegar solution. Apply a little bit at a time, blotting frequently with a dry cloth until the stain disappears.

5 Sponge with cold water and blot dry.

WINE, WHITE

FABRIC

1 Sponge the spot with cool water or soak for about 30 minutes in a basin of cool water.

2 Pretreat with prewash stain remover.

3 Launder with fabric-safe bleach.

UPHOLSTERY

1 Blot up as much of the spilled wine as possible.

2 Mix 1 tablespoon hand-dishwashing liquid and 1 tablespoon white vinegar with 2 cups cool water.

3 Using a clean white cloth, sponge the stain with the detergent/vinegar solution.

4 Blot until the liquid is absorbed.

5 Repeat Steps 3 and 4 until the stain disappears.

6 Sponge with cold water and blot dry.

CARPET

1 Blot up the spilled wine.

2 Mix 1 tablespoon hand-dishwashing liquid and 1 tablespoon white vinegar with 2 cups warm water.

3 Using a clean white cloth, sponge the stain with the detergent/vinegar solution. Apply a little bit at a time, blotting frequently with a dry cloth until the stain disappears.

4 Sponge with cold water and blot dry.

PHOTO CREDITS

COVER
Front: Mike Garten
Spine: Kate Sears
Back: © Jane Beiles: (upper right), © Rachel Boling (lower left), © Eric Roth, (lower right)

INTERIOR
Courtesy All-Clad: **45**
Chris Bain: **47** (bottom left)
© Jane Beiles: **52**
© Petra Bindel **107**
Courtesy Bosch Home Appliances: **60**
© Stacey Brandford: **34**, **113**
Courtesy Bissell: **19** (bottom right), **53**
Courtesy Black and Decker: **19** (top right), **43**
© Rachel Boling: **8**
Courtesy Clopay: **136**
Courtesy Clorox: **115** (bottom)
Courtesy Container store: **79**, **134**, **138**, **139** (left)
Corbis: **66**
Courtesy Cuisinart: **43**
© Roger Davies: **124**
Depositphotos.com: © Elnur Amikishiyev **21**, © Rashad Ashurov (stopwatch), throughout © Belchonock **9**, © bioraven (cleaning icons) throughout, © Bjphotographs **24** (bottom), © Natasha Fedorova **19** (left) © Maxim Ibragimov **15**, © Netkoff (cleaning icons) throughout, © Vitalytitov **26**, © Willeecole **58**
© Trevor Dixon: **162**
© Hotze Eisma: **122**

© Dana Gallagher: **2**, **4** (top left)
© Gallery Stock: **56**
Mike Garten: **ii**, **7**, **13**, **42**, **46**, **94**, **95**, **152**, **157**
Getty Images: © AE Pictures Inc. **88**, © Gary Alvis **144** (right), © Andresr **18**, © Carolyn Barber **12**, **109**, © Bill Boch **70**, © Steve Brown Photography **23**, © Linda Burgess **141**, © Caiaimage/Sam Edwards **143**, © Comstock Images **147** (left), © Jeffrey Coolidge **121**, © Chateau Dede **67**, © DNY59 **188**, © Robert Daly **38**, © Newton Daly **145**m © Sara Danielsson **47** (top right), © Floortje **175**, © Fotografia Basica **39**, © Fotostorm **49**, © Glow Décor **25**, © Steve Gorton **170**, © Jamie Grill **159**, © Alex Hayden **4** (bottom right), **148**, © Hero Images **69**, **73**, **90**, **131**, © Image Source **68**, **101**, © Ruth Jenkinson **65**, © JGI/Tom Grill **108**, © Julichka **180**, © Sean Justice **125**, © Dorling Kindersley **61**, © Rick Lew **86**, © Rick Lew/Digital Vision **135** (right), © Mark Lund **24** (top), © Charles Maraia **127**, © MartiVig **179**, © Maskot **6**, © Mellemrum/GAP Interiors **98**, © ML Harris **36**, © Montreal Photos **76**, © Moodboard **10**, © Mother Image **62**, © Multi-bits **100**, © Steven Mark Needham **173**, © Nick M Do **178**, © Oonal **135** (left) © Pattanan Umpornchaichote / EyeEm **146**, © Pbombaert **193**, © Lauri Patterson **70**, © PeopleImages **105**, © Jo-Ann Richards **85**, © Lew Robertson **174**, © Francesca Russell **126**, © Henrik Sorensen **74**, © Spaces Images **51** (top), © Tamara Staples **103**, ©Tetra

INDEX

A

Acetone, for stain removal, 150

Alcoholic beverages, stain removal, 158, 193

Alcohol (rubbing), uses, 129. *See also* Stain removal guide

Allergen protection, 21, 87

Ammonia, for stain removal, 150

Apple juice or applesauce, stain removal, 158–160

B

Baking soda
about: uses of, 22
fighting odors, 26, 33, 49, 131
for floors, 53, 98
freshening stuffed animals/fabrics, 25, 85, 131
for glassware, 45
in refrigerator, 33
for stove, 31

Barbecue sauce, stain removal, 160

Bathroom, 111–131
avoiding bar soap, 119
cell phone in, 121
cleaners for, 17
cleaning calendar (daily, weekly, occasional), 12
cleaning in minutes, 112–114
cleaning wipes for, 112, 116
clutter-free counter, 117
cosmetics storage, 120
dryer sheets for cleaning up, 119
fan, use and maintenance, 121
flushing toilet, 120

linen closet cleanup, 130–131
making things gleam (mirrors, faucets, etc.), 113
medicine cabinet makeover, 128–129
mistakes to avoid, 120–121
mold/mildew control, 14, 124–125, 126
organizing and organizers, 117, 122–123, 128–131
scents, 114
shaking out rug, 114
shower curtain care, 117, 124
squeegeeing your shower, 116
toilet bowl cleaners, 17, 119
toilet cleaning tips, 112, 113, 115
toothbrush storage, 120
towel bars, 118, 124, 130
towels, 115, 127, 131
toys, cleaning, 126
tub/shower cleaning tips, 115, 116–117, 118
ultra speed-cleaning, 115
under-sink storage, 123
water repellent for shower walls/doors, 118

Bedrooms, beds, and linens
allergen protection, 87
dusting wisely, 83, 102–103
fast fixes for, 82–83
floor care, 83
folding fitted sheets, 88–89
guestroom prep, 90–91
kid's rooms cleanup, 92–93
luggage rack in, 91
making beds, 82
mattress, bedding care, 84–85
pillow care, 68–69, 86–87

pillowcase uses, 87
putting everything away, 82
refreshing bed, 90
stain-removal tips, 84. *See also* Stain removal (for carpet, fabric, upholstery)

Berries, stain removal, 160–162. *See also* Strawberries

Blanchett, Cate, 55

Blender, cleaning, 42

Blinds, cleaning/caring for, 104, 105

Blood, stain removal, 162

Blueberries, stain removal, 160–162

Bombeck, Erma, 111

Bubble gum, stain removal, 163

Butter, stain removal, 162–163

C

Cabinets
cleaning frequency, 51
kitchen, 50–51
medicine cabinet makeover, 128–129

Calendar for cleaning, 10–13

Candle wax, stain removal, 164

Car, cleaning/washing, 146–147

Carpets
deep-cleaning options, 101
stain-removal guidelines, 100, 157. *See also* Stain removal (for carpet, fabric, upholstery)
stopping stains from reappearing, 100
vacuuming, 83

Cast iron, preserving, 45

Chewing gum, stain removal, 163

Chocolate, stain removal, 165

Cleaning basics, 3–27
calendar for cleaning, 10–13
decluttering before cleaning, 5
habits to adopt, 4–9
having "house only" shoes, 7
keeping supplies handy, 4
letting cleaner do the work, 8
no no's to avoid, 9
working top to bottom, 6

Cleaning materials
foaming cleaner benefits, 9
must-have cleaners, 16–17
must-have tools, 14–15
no no to avoid, 9
organizing, 47
pantry staples that clean too, 22

Closets, organizing, 78–79, 91, 92–93, 130–131. See also Linen closet

Clothing care. See also Ironing; Laundry
ironing mistakes to avoid, 74–75
stain removal. See Stain removal (for carpet, fabric, upholstery)
storage tips, 78–79

Clutter, removing
bathroom counter, 117
before cleaning, 5
of cleaning supplies, 48
in family rooms, 94–95

Coffeemaker, cleaning/maintaining, 41

Coffee, stain removal, 165

Comforters, washing, 68–69

Computers, cleaning/organizing, 108–109

Congran, Shirley, 3

Cooking oil, stain removal, 167

Cookware, cleaning, 44–45

Cranberry sauce stains, 160–162

Crayons, stain removal, 167–168

Curtains and drapes, cleaning/caring for, 105

D

Dent, James, 133

Desk organization. See Office

Diller, Phyllis, 29

Dirt, stain removal, 168. See also Mud

Dishes, detergents for, 17

Dishwasher, cleaning, 36–37

Disinfecting wipes, 16

Drapes and curtains, cleaning/caring for, 105

Drink stains. See Stain removal (for carpet, fabric, upholstery)

Dry cleaning, 62–63

Dryer sheets, reusing, 119

Dryer, vacuuming, 73. See also Laundry

Drying clothes, 61, 67

Dusters, 15, 102

Dusting, 83, 84, 91, 97, 102–103. See also Vacuuming

Dust mites, 85

E

Egg, stain removal, 168–169

Enzyme presoaks, for stain removal, 150

F

Fabric, removing stains from. See Stain removal (for carpet, fabric, upholstery)

Family rooms
cleaning calendar (daily, weekly, occasional), 13
clutter fixes, 94–95
fireplace cleaning, 144
furniture layout, 94
speed-cleaning tips, 96–97
tabletop organization, 95
vacuuming, 97

Feces, stain removal, 169

Felt-tip marker, stain removal, 169–170

Fireplace, refreshing, 144

Floors. See also Vacuuming
all-in-one multi-surface cleaner, 53
cleaners for, 17, 53
kitchen, 31
wood, mistakes to avoid, 99
wood, spiffing up, 98

Foundation (liquid makeup), stain removal, 176–177

Fruit punch, stain removal, 170–171

Fur, collecting, 26

Furniture
bathroom organizers, 122–123
dust removal, 97
layout of, traffic flow and, 94
outdoor, 140
polish/polishing, 17, 83, 107
removing moisture rings from wood, 103
storage built into, 95

Furniture, continued
  upholstery cleaning, 96.
    See also Stain removal
    (for carpet, fabric,
    upholstery)

G

Garage
  cleaning out/washing car,
    146–147
  oil stain removal, 136
  organizing, 134–135, 137,
    138–139
  pegboard storage, 138
  plain-sight storage, 139
  recycling areas, 139
  shelving for, 138
  storing dangerous goods,
    137
  sweeping out, 136
  things to remove from, 137
Germs, killing, 16, 17, 30, 41,
  48–49, 120–121
Glass multisurface cleaner,
  16
Glassware, de-gunking, 45
Gloves, rubber, 15
Grape juice, stain removal,
  171
Grass, stain removal, 172
Gravy, stain removal, 171–
  173
Grease, stain removal, 173
Grill cleaning and use,
  142–143
Gum, stain removal, 163
Gutters, cleaning, 144

H

Hydrogen peroxide, uses,
  129. *See also* Stain removal
  (for carpet, fabric,
  upholstery)

I

Ice cream, stain removal,
  173–174
Ink (ballpoint), stain
  removal, 174
Ironing
  mistakes to avoid, 74–75
  when to iron, when to
    steam, 76–77
  wrinkle releaser for, 77

J

Jelly, stain removal, 174–175

K

Ketchup, stain removal, 175
Keyboards, de-gunking, 108
Kids
  cleaning their toys, 24, 25,
    87, 126
  cleaning up after, 24–25,
    92–93
Kitchen, 29–53
  about: 30-minute clean-
    up tips, 30–31
  cabinet upkeep, 50–51
  cleaners for, 17
  cleaning calendar (daily,
    weekly, occasional), 11
  cookware, 44–45
  countertops, 30
  decluttering cleaning
    supplies, 48
  exhaust fan tip, 51
  floor, 31, 53
  killing germs, controlling
    odors, 48–49
  sink area organization, 31,
    46–47
  table, 30
  trash disposal, 47
Kitchen appliances,
  cleaning, 32–43
  about: wiping down, 31

blender, 42
coffeemaker, 41
dishwasher, 36–37
microwave, 39
range and stove-top, 31,
  35–36
refrigerator, 33
toaster oven, 43

L

Laundry. *See also* Stain
  removal (for carpet,
  fabric, upholstery)
  about: cleaning washer
    and dryer, 73; laundry
    room upkeep, 72–73;
    storing products for, 72
  colors bleeding in, 66
  delicate items/cycles, 57
  dry cleaning and, 62–63
  drying tips, 61
  frequency of washing (by
    item), 60–61
  hand-washing instead of
    dry cleaning, 63
  hand-washing mistakes to
    avoid, 64–65
  minimizing wrinkles, 61
  mishaps, fixing, 66–67
  pillows and comforters,
    68–69, 87
  prepressing, 61
  presorting, 56
  pretreating, 57
  products (detergents,
    pretreaters, softeners,
    bleaches), 59
  shrinkage fix, 67
  sorting strategies, 58
  stopping paring, 56
  stuffed animal care, 25, 87
  tissues left in, 66
  towels, 127
  vinyl shower curtain, 126
Lemon juice, uses of, 22, 39
Lighting, dust removal, 91

Linen closet, organizing, 88, 130–131

Lint rollers, 24, 66, 96, 146

Lipstick, stain removal, 175–176

Living room. *See* Family rooms

Lotion, stain removal, 176. *See also* Suntan lotion

Luggage rack, 91

M

Makeup, stain removal
lipstick, 175–176
liquid, 176–177
mascara, 177

Marker, felt-tip, stain removal, 169–170

Mascara, stain removal, 177

Mattress, caring for, 85

Medicine cabinet makeover, 128–129

Microfiber cloths, 14

Microwave, 39

Milk, stain removal, 177–179

Mold/mildew, controlling, 14, 124–125, 126

Mop, buying and uses, 15

Mud, stain removal, 179. *See also* Dirt

Mustard, stain removal, 178

N

Nail polish, stain removal, 179–180

Nonstick pans, cleaning, 45

O

Odor elimination
in car, 147
kitchen, 48–49
linen closet, 131
mattress, 85
pet smells, 26

Office, 106–109
bulletin board/magnetic strips, 107
cleaning screens, 108
de-gunking keyboards, 108
labeling items, 107
maximizing space, 106
organizing desktop, 109
shredding documents, 106
weeding out old devices, 109

Oil (cooking), stain removal, 167. *See also* Salad dressing, stain removal

Oil (garage). stain removal, 136

Orange/juice, stain removal, 180

Outdoors
furniture, cleaning, 140
grill cleaning and use, 142–143
gutter cleaning, 144
patio, porch, deck spruce-ups, 140–141
window cleaning, 9, 144, 145

P

Paint (latex/acrylic), stain removal, 180–182

Paint (oil-based), stain removal, 182

Paper towels, buying and uses, 15

Paperwork, purging, 98

Paquin, Anna, 149

Pencil lead, stain removal, 182–183

Perfume, stain removal, 183

Perspiration, stain removal, 183–184

Petroleum jelly, uses, 129

Pets, cleaning up after, 26. *See also* Feces, stain removal; Urine, stain removal; Vomit, stain removal

Pillowcase uses, 87

Pillows, cleaning/caring for/replacing, 68–69, 86–87

Pine resin, stain removal, 184

Polishing furniture, 17, 83, 103

Pollen, stain removal, 184–185

Poop, stain removal, 169

Pots and pans, 44–45

Q

Quotes on cleaning
Blanchett, Cate, 55
Bombeck, Erma, 111
Congran, Shirley, 3
Dent, James, 133
Diller, Phyllis, 29
Paquin, Anna, 149
Rivers, Joan, 81

R

Range and stove-top, 31, 35–36

Raspberries, stain removal, 160–162

Recycling areas, 139

Refrigerator, 33

Rings (moisture), removing from wood, 103

Rivers, Joan, 81

Rust remover, 150

Rust, stain removal, 185

S

Salad dressing, stain removal, 186

Salt, uses of, 22

Sap stains. *See* Pine resin, stain removal

Scrubbers, buying and uses, 15

Shades, cleaning/caring for, 104, 105

Sheets, folding fitted, 88–89

Shoe polish, stain removal, 185–187

Shoes, taking off at entry, 7

Shredding documents, 106

Sink, kitchen, 46–47

Soft drinks, stain removal, 187

Soy sauce, stain removal, 187–188

Spaghetti sauce, stain removal, 188

Squeegees, 14

Stainless steel appliances, cleaners/cleaning, 14, 17, 31, 33

Stainless steel pans and utensils, cleaning/shining, 45

Stain removal (for carpet, fabric, upholstery)

about: carpet care guidelines, 100, 157; drying clothes with stains, 67; essential supplies for, 150–151; golden rules of, 70–71; Good Housekeeping online reference for, 150; pet stains, 26; stopping stains from reappearing, 100; techniques (blotting; sponging; scraping, tamping, presoaking, freezing, flushing), 153–154; upholstery cleaning codes (W, S, WS, X), 156

alcoholic beverages, 158, 193

apple juice or applesauce, 158–160

barbecue sauce, 160

berries, 160–162. *See also* strawberries

blood, 162

butter, 162–163

candle wax, 164

chewing gum, 163

chocolate, 165

coffee, 165

cooking oil, 167

crayon, 167–168

dirt, 168. *See also* mud

egg, 168–169

feces, 169

felt-tip marker, 169–170

fruit punch, 170–171

grape juice, 171

grass, 172

gravy, 171–173

grease, 173

ice cream, 173–174

ink (ballpoint), 174

jelly, 174–175

ketchup, 175

lipstick, 175–176

lotion (hand, facial, body), 176

milk, 177–179

mud, 179. *See also* dirt

mustard, 178

nail polish, 179–180

orange/juice, 180

paint, latex (acrylic/water-based), 180–182

paint, oil-based, 182

pencil lead, 182–183

perfume, 183

perspiration, 183–184

pet stains. *See* feces; urine; vomit

pine resin, 184

pollen, 184–185

rust, 185

salad dressing (creamy/vinaigrette), 186

shoe polish, 185–187

soft drinks, 187

soy sauce, 187–188

spaghetti sauce, 188

strawberries, 188–189

suntan lotion, 189

tape (adhesive residue), 189–190

tea, 190

tomato/juice/paste/sauce, 190–191

urine, 191–192

vomit, 192–193

wine (red and white), 193

Static, controlling, 59, 77, 105

Steamer, using, 77

Storage

bathroom. *See* Bathroom

closet, 78–79, 91, 92–93, 130–131. *See also* Linen closet

clothing/fabric, 78–79

garage, 134–135, 137, 138–139

for kids' rooms, 92–93

linen closet, 88, 130–131

putting everything away, 82

shared-room, 93

Strawberries, stain removal, 188–189

Stuffed animals, freshening, 25, 87

Suntan lotion, stain removal, 189

T

Tape (adhesive residue), removing, 189–190

Tea, stain removal, 190

Toaster oven, cleaning, 43

Toilet bowl cleaner, 17

Tomato/juice/paste/sauce, stain removal, 190–191

Tools (cleaning), must-have, 14–15
Towel bars, 118, 124, 130
Towels, 115, 127, 131
Toxic goods, storing, 137
Toys, cleaning, 24, 25, 87, 126
Trash disposal, kitchen, 47. *See also* Recycling areas

U

Upholstery cleaning codes, 156. *See also* Stain removal (for carpet, fabric, upholstery)
Urine, stain removal, 191–192

V

Vacuum cleaners
buying recommendations, 15, 19
canister, 19
changing bag, 21
cleaning brush roll, 21
handheld, 19
maintenance tips, 21
mini vacs, 53
rewinding cord, 21
robot, 19
stick, 19
types and uses, 19
washing/changing filter, 21
Vacuuming
bare floors, 9
bedrooms, 83
dryer, 73
fabric/upholstery, 84
family rooms, 97
strategy, 83
Vinaigrette, stain removal, 186
Vinegar, distilled white
about: uses of, 22
cleaning dishwasher, 37
cleaning iron, 75
cleaning microwave, 39
deodorizing with, 48
de-scaling coffee maker, 41
stain removal with. *See* Stain removal (for carpet, fabric, upholstery), *specific stains*
stripping softeners from fabrics, 127
Vomit, stain removal, 192–193

W

Wall doodles, cleaning, 24
Washer, cleaning, 73. *See also* Laundry
Wax, stain removal, 164
Window covering, cleaning, 104–105
Windows, washing/cleaning, 9, 144, 145
Wine (red and white), stain removal, 193
Wipes, disinfecting, 16
Wood floors. *See* Floors
Wood, removing moisture rings from, 103

HEARSTBOOKS

An Imprint of Sterling Publishing Co., Inc.
1166 Avenue of the Americas
New York, NY 10036

ISBN 978-1-61837-248-2

Hearst Communications, Inc. has made every effort to ensure that all information in this publication is accurate. However, due to differing conditions, tools, and individual skills, Hearst Communications, Inc. cannot be responsible for any injuries, losses, and/ or damages that may result from the use of any information in this publication.

Distributed in Canada by Sterling Publishing
c/o Canadian Manda Group, 664 Annette Street
Toronto, Ontario, M6S 2C8, Canada
Distributed in Australia by NewSouth Books
45 Beach Street, Coogee, NSW 2034, Australia

For information about custom editions, special sales, and premium and corporate purchases, please contact Sterling Special Sales at 800-805-5489 or specialsales@sterlingpublishing.com.

Manufactured in China

2 4 6 8 10 9 7 5 3 1

sterlingpublishing.com
goodhousekeeping.com

Cover design by Scott Russo
Interior design by Susan Welt
For photo credits, see page 194